*This book is dedicated with love and gratitude
to my mother, Helena Harlow Worthen
and Grandmother, Eleanor Goddard Worthen*

CONTENT:

ACKNOWLEDGMENTS

It was late one night in May of 1995. I had been working on this book for four months, and had flown to Virginia, from California, to meet with Beverly's family, primarily her parents, Ed and Doreen. They had collected several boxes containing Beverly's letters, articles and news clips about her, and her accomplishments. Doreen had gone to bed, and Ed Johnson and I were finishing sorting through the letters. We sat at the kitchen table with the overhead light shining down on us, illuminating the table, strewn with Bev's history.

I noticed one piece of white paper, no envelope, folded in quarters, and picked it up. I realized, without having to read it, what I held. I had heard from Beverly's close friends of her practice of keeping a note written to her parents inside her passport in case she was killed. I had not expected to find the letter, much less in this pile. I handed it to Ed and asked if I could read it. "Yes," he replied. I read the letter through, then looked at Ed. The light made his face seem old and worn out, exhausted by more than lack of sleep. His expression was removed, his eyes, stoic.

"Did it help?" I asked. "Did this letter make her death any easier?"

"No." He answered without pausing. "Not one bit."

In those four words lay all the anger and frustration of a man whose only daughter was gone, not off to some exotic and remote place but to somewhere where her voice, her smile, her hugs, would never be with him again.

What struck me in his reply was the futility of story telling in the light of this kind of loss, and the selfishness of exploration and adventure. I remember once I had told my mother of a near miss in the mountains. I was shocked when she began to cry as she listened to me. The story she heard was not of an exciting glorious escape from death but rather of her little girl in danger.

In climbing stories we often magnify our adventures, creating legends and myths, providing ourselves with examples of courage and heroism. But for family and friends, and the audience beyond the climbing community, these stories can be shattering and devastating examples, which only demonstrate their own helplessness in the face of our pursuits for glory or fulfillment.

It was the anger of this futility that I saw in Ed Johnson's eyes that night—that this piece of paper, a letter in which Bev explained how much she felt she had received in her life and how grateful she was, was still all he had left of his daughter, and of couse it did not help a damn bit.

How secondary the stories are to the presence of the person. There is the myth and then there is the reality. Making the myth is important, but when we step into the myth to make more of our lives, we miss what the effect of this may be on the people who love us regardless of what the legend we leave behind.

Beverly understood this and was not consumed by the epic of her life. Her letter concludes this book.

Before starting this project I was acquainted with the legend Beverly Johnson, but not the person. Twenty-four years my senior, Bev's climbing fueled my generation's dreams, but not our reality. Over the past year, however, I have had the privilege of getting to know who Bev was beyond what she did. In this task I have been guided, aided and encouraged by many people without whom this book would not exist.

My sincerest gratitude goes to Beverly's family, and especially to her parents, Ed and Doreen, who all opened their lives and their homes to me and shared with me the Beverly they love.

The number of Beverly's friends who helped me is too long to list here. Notably, MJ Koreiva, Ron Peers, and Janet Kellum all gave considerable time to push this project forward. Michael Graber's contributions and his willingness to aid in the creation of this book is a testament to the sort of love Bev inspired.

Steve Roper's editorial advice and support and Gilberto's faith have also been invaluable.

Finally, my own family and friends: my father, Alyosha, my step-parents Liisa and Joe and my grandmother Eleanor contributed their loving kindness and well honed editorial advice.

My mother deserves a long sauna and swedish massage.

Last of all, for the serenity they have given me through innumerable storms, thank you thank you, Alice, Jennifer, Karen, Scout and H.P.

Beverly Johnson

FOREWORD

The front pages of the *Los Angeles Times* carried the story, that along with Frank Wells (president of Disney Productions) and two others, Beverly Johnson, of Jackson Hole, Wyoming, had died in a helicopter crash. I've lost many friends to high mountains, steep rocks, deep caves, and the like, but this grim news had never so violently ripped the wind from my chest as in reading this article. Of course, I'd never considered Beverly's death, but somewhere deep I believed that her end would resemble the conclusion of a classic play, where the principal persons still act in character. For the first hour after reading the article, I didn't know who I was. This play was not well-written. It was grotesque and hateful. The author deserved to be shot.

Over the next few months, as I talked with her husband (the crash's only survivor, and recovering from serious injuries), I couldn't shake a concept that I'd read in a book review—that all great people must be forgotten. I've only come across a few ideas that seemed like wisdom and crap at the same time, and this was one of them. But the idea wouldn't go away, nor would the thousand reasons I never want to forget Beverly.

Beverly Johnson was famous when I first went to Yosemite Valley as a wannabe rock climbing star in the spring of 1971. I didn't know that I had the tools to become a formidable climber, but several resident icons did, and I was taken into their inner circle much as a family takes in a stray dog. In 1971, Yosemite Valley was the *sanctum sanctorum* of world rock climbing, and the Yosemite climbers were the best. Several of the inner circle had international reputations; all of them stayed in Camp 4, traditional outdoor flophouse for anyone with the dream, a rope and a restless spirit.

Back then, the finest climbers were all dirt poor, a fact illustrated by Camp 4 itself. Beyond a gravel parking lot rested dozens of colorful tents, scattered like a fistful of jelly beans over a patch of dark forest. Official campsites were marked with a number stenciled on a splintered picnic table, but there was never anybody to enforce these things. The Park Service considered Camp 4 the biggest Babylon of rogues in California, and had essentially roped the place off. Only climbers stayed there. With no rangers and no rules, we were in hog heaven. The whole place was an international ghetto. And amongst the rabble from all ports, dead center in the inner circle, was Beverly Johnson.

Though only in her early twenties, Beverly had climbed with all the greats, had taken part in historic first ascents, and would shortly complete the first all-female ascent of El Capitan, the crown jewel of world rock climbing, and ultimate goal of all climbers. In 1971, Beverly Johnson was already a legend, but you'd have never known it had you met her then. Through my eyes she seemed totally out of place. With the lithe, muscular body of the gymnast she'd once been, she radiated a rich femininity that was a grace note in contrast to all the intense male bluster we lived around and the stark conditions we lived in.

Like the few remarkable people I have met, Beverly enchanted me not with what she had done, and would go on to do, rather by who she was, and how she made me feel about myself. I remember tweaking my shoulder and having to stay off the rocks for a week. I'd spent the summer rounding into shape for a couple of big ascents, and now found myself winged and probably having to return to the college grind without bagging the climbs I'd spent the previous year thinking about, working out for and banking on for dream fodder. I was so bitter and cranky that for several days my best friends had avoided me. Then one morning Beverly came over to my campsite and started asking me about my shoulder, and about all the climbs I'd done that summer; many of which I'd never imagined doing the previous year. She asked me about school and the courses I was going to take. She made me breakfast while we talked. Slowly, she restored my enthusiasm for me, not simply for what I had done or hoped to do, and I came to realize I'd already had a season most climbers would kill for, myself included. I'd had enough for that year, but not 'til that morning did I know it, accept it, and celebrate—at Beverly's urging—the fantastic things I'd experienced the previous eighty days. Because Beverly was so grounded, so at peace with herself, she could slow even the most hyper of us down enough to smell the roses. A couple hours later, I packed up my old Volkswagen van and drove back to Los Angeles, feeling like God.

Twenty years later I'd understand that almost to a man (back then there was an excruciating lack of women in Camp 4), we'd all come from busted families, had been adopted, thrashed, tongue-lashed all of our lives and had fled to Yosemite because we'd been lucky enough to find something we were skilled at (climbing), and were literally dying to prove it. Unacknowledged rage and pain drove us up the finest rock climbs of the age. And then there was Beverly. Either her parents were saints, or she was a saint herself. We were coarse, selfish, hostile at times but mostly disenfranchised and proud of it. Unbelievably, Beverly was proud of us. When you try as desperately as we did to succeed, part of you doesn't believe in your own victories. You minimalize everything and exult in nothing but a chance to prove yourself all over again. But after my first ascent of El Capitan, Beverly met me with a giant smile and said she'd been watching us through binoculars and had never seen anything like it. "You guys have the fastest time up El Cap by over six hours. That's incredible." What else could I say but, "Yes, ma'am. It *was*."

Shortly after that I climbed Reed's Pinnacle with Beverly and afterward she said she'd never seen anyone climb so smoothly (I think she said as much to everyone she climbed with). We climbed Higher Cathedral Spire the next day and she told me the same thing. When I questioned her about overstating my case she said I kept getting better before her very eyes. I couldn't decide whether to smack her or kiss her. About a week later we were on the Glacier Point Apron. I was having an off day and fell several times on a route I'd normally walk up. When that debacle was over Beverly said she'd never had so much fun in her life. Her backside bore several nasty rope burns from holding my falls. "Scars of honor," she called them.

Hell, yes, I fell in love with her. I fell in love with her because we all fell in love with her. Nothing could have been more natural. And I don't mean in a romantic way, for in my case she was six years older when we first met, and the difference between a seventeen-year-old boy and a twenty-three-year-old woman is an age. I mean that I fell in love with who she was and how I felt around her. We all felt that way. Sometimes our regard toward her played out in goofy ways.

I remember a couple of us huddling over a *Playboy* magazine, our eyes out on stilts, when someone said, "Jesus, Beverly's coming!" We stashed the magazine—I think it was Canadian climber Hugh Burton who sat on it. Beverly came over and straightaway pulled the magazine out from under Hugh and we all flushed like a Sierra sunset as Beverly thumbed through the pages, pausing at the centerfold. "Jeepers," she said. "Looks like someone shot two rockets through the poor girl's back."

"We found it," I lied. "It was just laying here on the table."

"Say, Bev?" someone asked. "Does a woman's body really look like that?"

"This is a *really* sick place I live in." Beverly laughed. "You're all sick."

We told her that she looked better than every woman in the magazine and she called us all liars. We said that not one of those naked women could make their way up Leaning Tower or Mt. Watkins and Bev said that they all had better things to do. We told her that we loved her anyway and that she was twice the woman the models were and she gave us back the magazine and said we'd better look again.

I don't know what all Bev did after she left Yosemite. Nor do I care. When talented people stick with adventure long enough, they reach a level beyond which more mountains climbed and caves explored makes a difference in their standing. The top of the adventure ladder has never had many people and never will. Most people drop off before they accomplish the landmark achievements that distinguish them as the real deal, people who have forever changed the way we look at climbing, Arctic exploration, and so forth. Once you have done historic things—which Beverly certainly did— no one ever again questions your standing. The media will feast on your exploits, but the people atop the ladder hardly listen. What they care about is the person, and the fact that you are one of the few people on earth who can understand them. With Beverly Johnson, I feel all of us who grew up with adventure have lost someone who probably understood us better than we understand ourselves.

An image can live on in steel or marble, in photos, videos, books and memories, but the person goes with her last breath. Everything else is but an echo that one day gets lost in time. And yet something survives, something more real and personal than a statue or a requiem. And that something is carried on by all those who knew the person in flesh and blood and spirit.

I'd like to believe that Beverly's grace and compassion were larger than she was, and could never, should never be frozen in myths or celebrations. I do believe that this passion can be passed along the pageant of individual lives, and that each person can exhibit it to the extent that we love ourselves and each other. So long as the passion stays alive in us, and not merely in a statue or a book, there's always a chance that some other special person will come along through which the passion will find full expression and will light up every soul around.

In this ambiguous sense I can begin to understand that it is better to forget the person and to nourish the gift that she left to the living. It is a much better thing to tend to our lives and those around us than it is to deify her and, in effect, put her magic above the people who could use it most. I know this in my heart, and yet none of it can make me want to forget her, or believe my own words. I would much prefer the real thing. But I cannot have it. None of us can.

I try to picture Beverly in the Golden City, and I laugh. At first glance she would look as out of place as she seemed to me the first time I met her in Camp 4. But that's only my take on it. Any capable spirit could see that she belonged, that the stars were as much her place as the side of Half Dome, or the glare ice of Antarctica, or the jungles of Irian Jaya. So perhaps this play ended as it should. Perhaps Beverly is just where she needs to be. It's the rest of us who need to understand Beverly on her own terms, not ours. — *John Long*, December, 1995

Beverly Johnson. A Mike Hoover photo.

"...ONE BITE AT A TIME"

Beverly Johnson was enjoying the day. She was alone, thousands of feet above the Yosemite Valley floor, surrounded by acres of granite rock. A nomad in a vertical wilderness, she carried all she needed for her travels in the canvas bag she hauled behind her up the rock.

Perched high on the 3,000 foot face of the El Capitain formation Bev had arisen that morning, only after the sun warmed her sleeping bag cocoon anchored to the rock face. "I am a lizard," she said enjoying the warmth of the sun. And she could climb the rock as well as one would.

It was Monday, the 17th of October, 1978 when she started her solo climb of El Cap. El Capitan is an ocean of vertical grey and white rock. Petrified waves of stone create sweeping overhanging arches. Cracks like rivulets, some as wide as a thumbnail, some big enough to sleep in, stream down the face.

Bev had chosen the *Dihedral Wall* route up El Cap for her solo climb and as she climbed higher, the trees below slowly lost their form and soon the forested Valley looked like only a swipe of green paint with dashes of grey asphalt. At that time of year in Yosemite Valley the ground is covered with a soft rug of fresh pine needles, and at places the Merced River is only a trickle, with the spring thaw long past. After sunset the lights on the cars circling the Valley floor reminded Bev that though she was suspended in her own nylon solitude, the overpopulated Valley was not gone for good. Where waterfalls plummet over the lip of the Valley in the spring, in the autumn, dark swaths of mossy granite, giant black brush strokes streak down the walls. The naturalist John Muir declared Yosemite "the grandest, most divine of all earthly dwelling places." A later climbing writer,

Steve Roper called it a "small Shangri-La, one of the most beautiful spots of our planet," and Bev had a literal bird's eye view of it all.

What she saw was her home. She had been climbing for over twelve years, and had lived seasonally in Yosemite for over six. In addition to doing shorter climbs she had spent enough time on the walls in Yosemite to earn herself the nickname, "Big Wall Bev." Before this solo climb of El Cap in 1978 she had been most famous for completing the first ascent of El Capitan by a woman swinging leads (when each of the two partners take turns leading up the route), on the *Nose* with Dan Asay in 1973, and for completing the first all-women's ascent, on the *Triple Direct* with Sibylle Hechtel, also in 1973. Five days after that climb, she helped Charlie Porter—the visionary, and now legendary big wall solo climber—put up the El Cap classic, *Grape Race*. She was queen of the inner circle of climbing's highest echelon, and had swapped leads with the likes of Jim Bridwell, Steve Wunsch, Kim Schmitz, Barry Bates and John Long, all pioneering Yosemite rock climbers.

Yosemite's drama comes in part from the first startling view of the Valley which hits the visitors all at once. As you enter the Valley floor via highways 120 or 140, you must absorb simultaneously the delicacy of a wildflower and the grandeur of Half Dome and El Capitan. It is difficult to absorb or appreciate all this beauty at once, but rock climbers believe they have found a way.

Charlie Porter once wrote about Beverly's appreciation of for the magnificent eco-system of Yosemite; "Bev understood you can be living on a big rock face and enjoy it. She had an easy way of going about living; the rock cliff was her environment, she just lived there. . . ." By throwing themselves into the middle of the equation, rockclimbers participate in, rather than observe from afar, nature's tides and beauty. They live with nature's magnificence rather than analyze it.

Rock climbing in 1978, was still very much an activity on the society's fringe. Climbing was a rebel limb of alternative rugged outdoor sport, and to the few like Beverly, climbing was not a sport but a lifestyle. It was a life that included envisioning a week alone on three thousand feet of sweeping granite and calling a ledge on El Capitan home.

Bev had attempted to do this climb many times before but had been frustrated by weather and bad planning. This time, though, she was prepared to stay up there for as long as it took. Getting ready to climb a wall had, by this point in her life, become routine and a mental checklist of necessities was not hard to summon up. She would carry over a hundred pounds of gear including cheese, tuna fish, canned fruit, extra clothes, a sleeping bag, and water. Her haul bag, nicknamed "Piggy," served as her vertical pack mule although it was her muscle that would drag it up the rock behind her.

One slow pitch at a time, Bev would have to travel each rope length three times. She first climbed the pitch (one rope length of approximately 140 feet), placing her protection and repositioning her anchor each time she moved higher to belay (protect) herself in case of a fall. At the top of each rope length she anchored her rope to the rock, descend the pitch, and then climbed it again to collect the gear she had left during her initial ascent. Reaching her top anchor again she would finally have to raise up her 100 pound haul bag using a pulley system connected to her anchor. Solo climbing is slow and arduous work, and required the mentality of the little engine that could.

"One night," Bev said "I kept thinking and thinking that the way you eat an elephant is one bite at a time."

As she climbed Bev would have to continually rotate her perspective, like changing so many lenses on a camera. She would focus first on the next crystal nubbin a foot away to use as a handhold, then on a recess in a crack an inch from her face where she could lodge her next piton, and then to a ledge hundreds of feet away, up to where the day's climbing would take her, and finally up to the horizon, maybe fifteen hundred feet to where she would hopefully arrive in the next several days. The last view required an arched back and good anchor.

Sometimes Bev would stop to read a book. At times she would sunbathe lying on the ledge like a rock nymph, with shiny brown eyes, wispy sun bleached hair, weathered tan skin, and gypsy gold hoop earrings. She later told one reporter she would often " . . . pendulum over and look at some bats, or watch the light on the walls."

With each rope length Bev moved more and more into the smooth gray granite landscape. In the direct sun the *Dihedral Wall* became a vertical Sahara, acres upon acres of hot rock. When night fell she would pull out her hammock, tie herself to the rock and cuddle into her nylon home. With darkness the temperatures plummeted and except for a few echoes from the Valley floor she was alone, hanging among the stars.

On the ninth day, after over thirty pitches, she reached Thanksgiving Ledge, a unique formation that snakes hundreds of feet across the face, just below the summit, and the worst was behind her. She held a little celebration and burned her socks.

When she reached the top, although she may have wanted a moment to sit alone and reflect on her accomplishment, she found herself instead instantly surrounded by reporters and cameramen eager for a juicy quote.

A reporter from the *San Francisco Chronicle* told her that two women had died the day before during the all-women's attempt on Annapurna in the Himalayas, led by Arlene Blum. Beverly had been asked to join that team but had turned Blum down, noting to her friends that she didn't have a lot of faith in the technical ability and experience of the team Blum was forming. She commented to the reporter, "It's so sad . . . but I guess those sad things happen. I guess that maybe I will die in the mountains myself."

It took her ten days to climb the wall. Her motivation had been in the journey, not the achievement. Beverly had chosen a life defined by the explorer's maxim, driven by the process of discovering rather than the triumph of discovery. But that life had hard edges. Though she had experienced ten days in the middle of a sea of rock blanketed by an ocean of sun and stars, she emerged on the summit smiling but exhausted, victorious but scarred.

"OH BOY, WHERE'S SOME DIRT!"

Beverly Johnson's ancestors had a knack for getting themselves in difficult situations. One Johnson family legend holds that Ashton Powell Johnson, born in 1820, declared he could be killed only by a bullet through his head, a prediction fulfilled not too many years later. In 1942, Beverly's maternal grandfather, Commander Robert P. McConnell, was commanding the navy's first aircraft carrier, the *Langley*, when it was sunk by Japanese bombers off the coast of Java. No sooner had Commander McConnell and his crew been rescued by another ship, however, than the rescue ship was pulverized by more enemy bombers. Though only 146 of the original *Langley* crew of 439 survived Commander McConnell lived and went on to become a rear admiral.

Her mother and father, Doreen McConnell and Edward Johnson, met under circumstances that seemed unlikely to lead to a lasting relationship. The young Navy officer arrived at Doreen's door with his suit covered in mud (from the truck which drove through the puddle next to his convertible), and blood (an unruly razor nick). Johnson worsened his chances even more by escorting young Doreen to a whorehouse with the reputation as the greatest shack-up joint in the West (he swore it looked like a quaint little restaurant from the outside).

But something must have clicked, or maybe Doreen took pity on poor Ed, because they survived their first date and were married. Their first child, Beverly Ann, was born in Annapolis, Maryland on April 22, 1947, while Ed was attending Naval post-graduate school.

Doreen was an inexperienced mother and had actually never held a baby before she had Beverly. When Doreen attempted to do mothering by the book, trying to follow the *Better Homes and Gardens* suggested daily schedule of naps and feedings, most often Doreen and Beverly simply wound up crying together.

Bev and her family, which as of 1949, included her brother, Edward Jr, lived the nomadic life of the military, moving from Washington state to Alabama, Rhode Island and finally to Virginia. The Johnsons moved nine times before Bev was in high school. Ed, who served in the Korean war, was transferred from the East coast to West and back again. Doreen and the children were often alone with their own battles to face.

Beverly, the blossoming flower

Once in 1949 when Ed was stationed on Whidby Island off the coast of Washington, their pipes froze solid in a freak snowstorm, and Doreen and the kids were reduced to brushing their teeth with pineapple juice.

As a young child Beverly was conscious of other's emotions and positioned herself as a protector or caretaker. Ed recalls a trip to the zoo when Bev was almost six:

At that time we didn't have batteries to power toys, it was all done by springs. You wind up the springs and the toys do what they're supposed to.

We're standing there looking at the monkey cage, watching the monkeys swing back and forth, and "Wow, whatdya think of that, Bev?" I said. She looked at me. "When do they wind them up?" she said.

I thought about that, because that's pretty funny for a little girl— she knew they didn't wind them up, and probably thought to herself, "Well, dad's not very smart and he would probably think it would be very funny if I asked a 'little girl' question." It was funny in several ways and pretty interesting upon reflection.

That Christmas on Whidby Island Bev asked Santa for a dump truck. Upon receiving it, revved to go she exclaimed, "Oh boy, . . . where's some dirt!" Doreen said (with a smile) in 1995 that she wanted her little girl to grow up and be a dainty housewife, but to her dismay, Beverly continued to dive into things, usually dangerous or dirty things, head first, playing football and sloping around in the mud. When the family moved to Virginia Beach in 1955 she and her brother lived a Huck Finn existence, crabbing and swimming and playing in the nearby DDT trucks. In Montgomery, Alabama they chopped down bamboo to make fishing poles for perch

Bev and brother Ted. Johnson's family album

and sunfish. In Warwick, Rhode Island, where the family moved in 1958, Ted watched his sister coming into her own:

> We had everything there, sailing and ice skating and hockey, the whole bit. We had woods and we went out fossil hunting and we went clamming with our toes in the Marianza Bay. Once we got hold of a tin crate and Bev and I caulked it up and took it to the pond with a bunch of our friends. We were all looking at it, wondering who would get in.
>
> Well, Bev got in it. It was real tippy as we pushed it away from the shore. She managed to get back but nobody else went in.

Young Ted saw himself as something of a bodyguard for Beverly. Once, in Virginia Beach, when Ted was in second grade and Bev was in the fourth, a big bully was harassing her on the school bus. Angered by watching his sister sit there and take the harassment, Ted went up and punched the guy right between the eyes.

Bev's own frustration came out in other ways. When the rear door window on the 1955 Ford station wagon wouldn't close to her satisfaction, she got back about fifteen feet, took a run at it, leaped up in the air and hit it with both heels. The door closed, and couldn't be opened again for about three weeks.

Both Beverly and Ted became competent sailors as children and the family spent much of its time together out sailing. Sailing gave Ted and Bev a different way to be out in the natural world, and again Bev's protective mothering instincts came out, as Ed details:

> One time we were sailing and we wanted to bring some conch shells back, so we found some and brought them up. "So what are you going to do with those, dad?" she said. "I am going to get the conches out and take the shells home," I replied.
>
> "Those shells have got live critters in them, dad!"
>
> I guess she was pretty disappointed in her dad, that he would get rid of a critter just to have the critter's house.

Bev thrived socially on the constant stream of new environments as the family moved every two years but her early education was somewhat erratic. An avid reader from an early age she loved the Nancy Drew series and admired the feats of Amelia Earhart. She leap-frogged through the traditional curriculum, and experienced a variety of schooling styles, missing whole sections of some subjects but repeating her Virginia history class three times. She learned to determine for herself what was valuable to her education and what was not worth her energy. If the subject sparked her interest, she was not afraid to research something by herself and try to learn on her own.

Ted explained:

> If people move they don't feel attached to anything. It's very easy to make new friends, but again you don't keep friends for a long time, so you pull the best out of people, all the time. You are always looking at the best side of people. Bev could always bring out the

best in anybody, and she would know their weaknesses as well. She became flexible from moving around.

In 1960, when Ted was 11 and Bev was 13, they moved for the last time and settled in Arlington, Virginia. Ed retired, in part to allow the children to stay in one place throughout high school. A year later Bev's second brother Randy was born. While settling down ended her geographic exploration, it allowed Bev to concentrate on stretching in other ways.

During the junior high school years Bev had started taking gymnastics. By the time the Johnsons moved to Virginia where she enrolled at Yorktown High School, she was good enough to make the team. She became a true gym rat, spending hours each day working out. Gymnastics did not come naturally to her, but she was determined and would stay at the gym until she had perfected any move that gave her trouble. The combination of the intellectual focus and the physical challenge of gymnastics kept her intensely involved in the sport throughout high school.

Beverly had the ability to focus, concentrating on one sequence or on one move at a time, to the point of becoming a threat to her own health. Once, after finishing a difficult routine on the parallel bars in perfect form, she walked back across the gym, tripped over the mat, fell, and broke her arm.

Beverly at about 15 years of age. Johnson's family album photo.

Beverly treated her injuries more as a nuisance than a serious impediment. When her arm had been out of the cast for not more than two weeks, she asked her parents if she could borrow the car to go visit her aunt in Long Island. They agreed, completely unaware that in actuality she intended to compete in the upcoming Eastern AAU Women's Gymnastics Championships. When Beverly returned she admitted everything, and explained that she was a little miffed because she had only placed second. The judges had marked her down because they could see that she was favoring one arm.

As her high school years came to an end, Bev could not escape completely into her jock identity. She finally submitted to her mother's wishes that she have a formal coming out. Though a reluctant debutante, Beverly Ann Johnson was presented to Virginia society decked out in a regal white dress, twenty-one button gloves and a glorious beehive hairdo.

In September of 1965, she left for Ohio and Kent State University, with a suitcase full of leotards, and the two rules of the Johnson household firmly etched in her brain. "One, always tell the truth, no matter what; and two, never cry no matter how bad it hurts."

Photo, reproduction from a undeterminate newpaper article. Courtesy of the Johnson family

"...TAKING TO THE HILLS..."

In the spring of 1966, Beverly's freshman year at Kent State, she wrote home to her parents:

> I have become very restless lately, taking to the hills when I ought to be hitting the books. Even when I hit the books my mind heads for the hills.

Though she made the Dean's List, Bev's letters lament her inability to focus on her studies, and are full of excited descriptions of gymnastics, sailing, and briefly track. Her biggest trouble with college life was not to get involved, but rather in choosing what *not* to do.

Her father had warned her before she left for school not to over-commit herself, but on September 22nd, she wrote home, "Lord, this place is crawling with all kinds of people and things to do. Dad was right—you can't [just] have at it—be selective. So I'm trying, but oh, those choices."

She didn't do so well at heeding her father's advice.

Student life included the anti-war protests that were just beginning, and Bev occasionally joined in the demonstrations, but Kent's reputation had not yet been stained with the blood of student protesters and the escalating war in Vietnam was not a daily concern of hers.

As a freshman at Kent her antics were centered in the gym. The Kent gymnastics team was impressive and while the atmosphere was more relaxed than in Yorktown, the workouts were more intense. Her teammates' ability made her more determined than ever to work hard and improve herself. After the first competition she secured a fifth place spot on the team.

An early in her sophomore year she joined the sailing program.

> I just got the big word, she wrote to her parents. Bill Parker
> and I are going to sail for Kent in Detroit next weekend. . . .
> we'll be the only ones from Kent, but there are five schools
> from Canada plus some regionals and I'm so excited I'm about
> to split a seam . . . I decided . . . that being a crew is too much
> work and I think I'd rather be a skipper, so I'm very glad to be
> sailing with Parker and I'm learning quite a few tricks.

She did get to skipper a boat at the regatta and though she came in
dead last, she declared it "the most satisfying thing I've ever done." She
studied *The International Yacht Racing Rules* and *Expert Dingy Sailing*
books. She skippered her boats into ninth and sixth place in a later race
and wrote home, "The Canadians thought it was funny, 'Hey, the Americans
have a lady skipper.' I felt sort of bad beating them . . . . Anyway it was
very fun, if not a birth by fire (make that ice)."

In contrast to gymnastics, where she was surrounded by and competing
against women, on the sailing team Bev was one of the few women com-
petitors. This was not a deterrent for her, simply another piece of the game
which had both positive and negative dimensions. She was soon nicknamed
"the bitch of Lake Michigan," but when asked why she was in such great
demand to sail with the boys, she replied, "Where else can you find a 130
pound strong boy?" and later wrote, "If gymnastics did nothing for me,
it's made me a very agile sailor."

Though she saw her own size as an advantage, Bev was frustrated by
the other women she sailed with, and seemed to take their incompetence
as a personal affront. She skippered one race with a woman whom she
described as a "Chem 160 97-pound weakling," who had never sailed before
and didn't know the racing rules. Bev spent the lunch break during the race
day convincing the coach to get her a crew with more substance in both
expertise and girth.

Bev herself was unclear of how she added her next sport to her reper-
toire, but in April of 1966 she wrote home despondently:

> . . . for some unknown reason, at the last minute I decided to
> try out for cheerleading and made Varsity alternate. Just what I al-

ways wanted to do fall and winter quarter on top of twenty hours [of classes], gymnastics, sailing, and all the other garbage I get suckered into doing. At any rate Rudy [her gymnastics coach] I think, is about to run me through with a parallel bar rail. Anyway, he may be able to get me out of it. "The only reason she tried out was she didn't think she was going to make it" I don't know. What a mess.

Bev's appetite for academics was just as big as for athletics. The first semester at Kent she took 17 units, a heavy load but one that was to become the standard, if not on the lighter side for her. She took many of her professors with a rather large grain of salt. In one letter she offered her parents a critique:

> Gym will go without comment. Ten o'clock is English (A.P. gads) . . . "he who goofs the grammar fails the course . . ." From 1-3 is Art . . . We got a nice lecture on air (i.e. abstract meaning, what makes a painting great and the rest of the bull which sounds good in a studio but doesn't mean anything.) . . . Everybody is dead serious, even the instructor.
>
> At three is Geology under a Doctor Rau who told us about his childhood in South Dakota (which people started taking notes on) and how he spends his summers in the Rockies. He made sure we didn't leave without knowing he holds a Ph.D. from Yale and something or other from Stanford.

In relations with men Bev also had a clear sense of her own boundaries, and beware those who crossed them.

One winter day she was wearing a wool ski cap and was walking to class when she heard a man behind her say, "I guess there's a cute girl under that ski cap and I'm going to take that ski cap off." She told him to shove off. After her class, though, he continued to follow her as she walked to her dorm to get her books. When she came out of her dorm he was waiting for her on the steps. As she walked by he pulled off her hat. She responded with a right hook to the jaw, which knocked him over backwards and down the steps. She walked down the steps, picked up her hat, stepped over his sprawled body and went to class.

The next afternoon when she returned to her room there was a note for her to report immediately to the dean of women, which she did. She was informed that she had broken the student's jaw. After explaining that he was six two, 220 pounds and harassing her, Bev was allowed to leave without a reprimand.

In 1966 collegiate women were expected to be focused on their search for a husband to the exclusion of other pursuits. But in romantic relationships Bev's biggest concern was that her suitors would get too serious and expect her to settle down. A gift of flowers from one admiring young man induced her to comment to her parents:

> The flowers are very pretty. I think he wants me to fix his dinner or something.

About another relationship she wrote:

> After four weeks I am trying to plot my course of action for my budding little relationship with Larry (this is a little hard to put in words.) But it seems like it's back to the old story—What do you do when a fellow who is a lot of fun, who you really admire, and is quite talented . . . starts showing tinges of getting serious? Spit in his eye? I never thought old Larry, who is an independent soul to the very core, would. Alas, another perfectly good relationship bites the dust. But what can you do? I can certainly live without any more debacles. I keep telling myself, I'm going to kick myself downstairs when I become a little old maid— (but not until then.)

However, Bev's spinster worries were unfounded and an addendum to her letter included the note, "Having given Larry the ax—yours truly, who will never learn, is back at it again." This time the poor fellow's name was Al and Bev hoped his intentions would maintain their frivolous path.

Beverly's college life was centered in athletics and outdoors activities, which formed the heart of her life on campus. Her letters again and again, while making note of academics and boys and friends, are most often full of detailed descriptions of her exploits in the gym and outdoors. Her first spring in Ohio she finds herself pushing her schoolwork aside in order to be outside. Despite her jaunts, she cannot subdue her energy and in a somewhat distressed letter home writes:

> I have not been able to shake my spring fever yet. I am out
> for track now too. I started off in running broad (please no
> puns) and high jump and sprints. I now find myself running the
> 440 and 880 because I have a "nice long stride." I also don't
> have any wind but I guess that isn't a consideration. Poor me,
> running is just dirty hard work. We have track practice from 4 or
> 4:30 to 6:00, dinner and gymnastics from 7 to 9:30 or so. I tried
> getting up at five-thirty to run in the mornings but after one run
> through the black and grey (and frigid) dawn, I decided to limit
> it to 4 to 6 in the afternoon.

Going sailing didn't seem to help her restlessness, possibly in part due to the frustrations she faced with Ohio weather, one of the greatest detriments to sailing at Kent. Describing an upcoming regatta in Ann Arbor she said:

> It's been snowing here for the past two days and I imagine it's
> worse in Michigan. Sailing when it's snowing is miserable, every-
> thing freezes including the skipper and crew. The washer at
> Lowry, my dormitory, will probably corrode away from all the
> salt laden gear . . . I dump into it. (You put salt on everything to
> keep it from freezing up but it doesn't work on people.)

She added in a postscript, "Please send any long johns or foul weather gear that you can spare . . ."

In her sophomore year Bev's tolerance for Kent's winters began to diminish and she wrote to her grandparents, "I must go brave the Siberian Wilderness and go to class."

It was around this time that Bev attended a regatta where the sailing team from UCLA was competing. One look at the UCLA team's suntanned faces made it clear to her that the sailing out West was a far cry from the "frostbite regattas" she was used to. That November she wrote home, "I have a lot of things to discuss with you all that can't be done through the mail or over the telephone," and by February of 1967 she thought she was on her way to UCLA.

In reality she had enrolled in the University of Southern California. She had gotten confused during the application process, and applied to the University of Southern California (in Los Angeles) rather than the University of California *at* Los Angeles and had not realized her mistake until after she had already been accepted at USC. The allure of California didn't change however, and with characteristic nonchalance, Beverly set off in the spring of 1967 to defrost in the golden state.

"SORRY I WORRIED YOU"

Bev was slow to tune in to California in the sixties, or at least that's what she told her parents, when she wrote home;

LSD and Mary Jane [marijuana] are the big things here. When someone mentions "taking a trip" all ears perk up. It took me a while to catch on.

Bev quickly nestled into her gym rat niche. Donning her leotard and heading for the gym brought on familiar responses:

I discovered the only thing better than being a sorority girl is being a squared away little jock (pardon the expression). The girls are very well turned out and spend many happy hours before the mirror and shopping, so a girl that has time to stand on her hands is cause for considerable comment.

Did I tell you the story of USC's really great Women's Gym Team? It's kind of what you might call in the early stages of development—just now as a matter of fact, I'm it. I'm not griping. I can't gripe too much. Everyone has been very very nice to me . . . I have free access to the gymnastics gym and work out with the men's team . . . . The only complaint I can really lodge is that the equipment is lousy—especially the beam, which has the sturdy rigid construction of a rickety saw horse (and about the same dimensions) . . . the makeshift unevens (I take one bar out of the P-bars, raise the other one and shove the whole mess an appropriate distance from the high bar It's scary as hell but it works) and the nonexistent free-X floor (I use a corner of the football field and lots of imagination.) I have come to the conclusion that gymnastics at USC taxes my brain more than my brawn.

Bev was flexing her brain plenty, taking, in addition to traditional English and history courses, German and oceanography. Bev flirted briefly with majoring in Cinema, but switched back to Geology, writing home, "To hell with Cinema, Rocks is where I belong." She took particular joy in working through mechanical problems, reworking engineering designs and attempting to invent better ones. She wrote:

> We went "oceanographing" a week ago last Wednesday. I got rather obsessed with the piston core drill—which has a catcher which works fine except for sand grains, which strain right back out. For about a week, I tried to find a solution, then I sort of lost interest or got discouraged—Anyway, all that remains is an unbelievable litter of cut-up milk cartons and wire (mostly hair pins). Some catchers wouldn't even close, others worked pretty well. They never got past the washroom sink but it sure gave me an appreciation for the complexity of simple problems. The funny thing was that simplest designs worked the best (of course my inept *origami* probably had something to do with it.) If I ever have the metal cutters, and time, I may progress to tin can models—a nice mental exercise, at any rate.

Bev's ingenuity proved valuable again as she went job hunting. In one letter she mentioned:

> The girl down the hall just came over. Good news, (I guess) Here's a wild one for a job—Chorus girl in Vegas. $200 a week for one to two shows a night—eight and midnight. . . It's for eight weeks and the routine is fixed so there aren't many rehearsals. As long as we don't go topless or bottomless (or both) it's a pretty easy $1600, *nicht wahr?*

The Science and Technology Museum offered her a less audacious job as a part-time guide for $2.05 an hour. She said, "So here I am getting a much better education at the museum than in classes and getting paid for it. A crash course in everything from Astro-physics to Zeta functions."

Classes and work did not infringe on Bev's time outdoors, and by the spring of 1968 she was an active member in the USC mountaineering club, The Trojan Peak Club. As a geology student in the late '60s she faced the sexist attitudes toward women in the sciences, as well as the scepticism many felt about having women working in the field. In the mountaineering world however, Bev's purchase of a new climbing rope assured her popularity as a partner. Being an attractive athletic girl didn't hurt either.

Mountaineering synchronized Bev's passions, demanding athleticism, as well as mental dexterity and ingenuity. It offered close personal relationships and the opportunity to enjoy the beauty and simplicity of the natural world. A letter she wrote home on May 27, 1968 glows with this synergy:

Dear Folks,

Briefly:
Trojan Peak was named in 1926 in honor of the club. It was climbed again in 1953.

The Trojan Peak Club (us) was planning to climb it again next week to plant a register on the summit.

Bruce and I thought it would be a classic joke to climb it two weeks early and plant a register and not say anything until we all climbed and "voila!"

I left a very detailed itinerary with my roommates as the route was extremely strenuous through trailless arid brush, across deep scree strewn gorges up the densely wooded George Creek, across more trackless scree and scrub forest to the base of the peak. From there the ascent up an ice couloir to the face itself (unclimbed as far as we knew.) When we left the last rocky marshy meadow, there began the dead world of ice and rock and a three thousand foot climb to the summit.

Bruce is a very experienced mountaineer and since we are both in excellent condition we thought we could make it in three days.

When we arrived in Lone Pine we discovered that the Whitney Portal Road had been dynamited for repairs and we would have a longer, (considerably longer) cross-country traverse than expected. After a day of 4th class rock climbing with fifty pound expedition packs, containing mostly hardware, pitons, carabiners, rope, and ice gear—parkas, crampons (strap on foot spikes) ice axes, snow gaiters and other necessary gadgets, we must have made all of four miles and decided to return to the car across the Valley floor.

We got to the floor just after dark and traversed to the car in the cold desert night. We got to Lone Pine and tried to call my roommates who were not there. I tried several friends, but on Friday night it's pretty hard. Finally I got Mike Hull, and Bruce and I returned to the mountains by Hogback Road whose ruts defy the imagination.

I drove as Bruce had cracked up from exhaustion and was behaving in the strange manner I was to observe in the next four days. He was wandering around insisting he could see Williamson, that we weren't at Hogback; I gave him several dramamines and he fell asleep.

The next day we traversed from Hogback to George Creek through the worst imaginable terrain. It was hot, maybe 100 we had to beat our way through dry prickly desert scrub. The mosquitoes clung around our sweating bodies. The air was still hot and dry. It was impossible to breath the stifling air without inhaling gnats and mosquitoes. They flew at our faces and in our eyes. We would often stop, choking on the dust and bugs. Our only relief was to continue on. We went up and down seemingly endless scree slopes. (Scree is a mixture of sand and small stones; if it has a high angle of repose a wrong step finds you at the bottom which happened to both of us several times. It's not so bad if you're headed down anyway, but if after much labor you get 3/4th of the way up and find yourself back at the bottom it begins to strain the vocabulary.)

We arrived at George Creek at four in the afternoon after more than ten hours of misery with no rest and a quart of water—the wind blowing down George took care of most of the mosquitoes and gnats—and the dense trees and reeds obscured the sun. So we had lunch and tried to wash off some of the scree that had come along for the ride and went on our way sometimes through dense foliage near the stream but mostly rock climbing on the walls that flanked the creek.

About 8:30 we started setting up camp by the stream. We found a great spot and had the only reasonable camp of the trip. Bruce built a huge fire and although we cooked dinner on the stove, we roasted marshmallows on the fire, sang songs, discussed Byzantine architecture and the climb of the next day.

We got up before dawn, broke camp in a hurry and spent the entire day climbing and scrambling to the base of the peak through some of the most beautiful country thinkable. Trojan Peak is set far back along the creek and was not visible until we reached the base. Suddenly Trojan and Williamson rose before us; huge masses of granite snow and ice.

We set up base camp at the edge of the tree line, built a fire and had freeze dried, dehydrated beef Stroganoff, water proofed our boots, organized what would go in our summit packs and what would be left at base camp.

The night at ten thousand feet was a bad one. The moon hung over the summit and the thoughts of the next day, the climb, finally the summit, made sleep difficult and the gusts that blew down the ice swept through the mummy bags and made sleep impossible. The hood on my bag wasn't functioning and that made matters worse.

We got up before dawn so as to get as far as possible on the snow before the sun made avalanches a problem. We had freeze dried dehydrated clam chowder (the label said it was clam chowder anyway.) It was pretty bad; my stomach wrapped around it three or four times in a tight little knot. We took hardware, rope, and other assorted goodies and some equipment for our inevitable bivouac. The morning went uneventfully except Bruce sank up to his neck a couple of times and had to save himself with his ice ax. I managed to cleat myself in the calf with a crampon. I led, and we made good time up the couloir. We rock climbed another 1500' up to a narrow ridge that we traversed on the ice. The exposure was fantastic. A slip meant a rapid descent of more than three thousand feet back to basecamp unless the other could drive in an ax and wrap the rope. Since we were tied together the consequences of failure were pretty severe.

We carefully chipped our way up without mishap and rock climbed the last nine hundred feet to the summit. We looked back at the basecamp. The sun was setting at our backs. We had ascended nearly four thousand feet in just less than fourteen hours over ice and middle 4th to middle 5th class technical rock. The air was thin, and the wind strong.

We placed the register in the rocks on the delicate rock needle that was the summit (13,960'). To the Southwest and North the Sierra spread before us, the jagged summits scratching at the sky, the ice on fire from the setting sun. Below us frozen lakes and lower peaks, and nowhere to the West, North or South, a tree, a blade of grass, or anything living, only in the desert behind us now engulfed in the darkness was anything alive. It was a dead land, and I was overwhelmed by it. I will never forget the sensation, the sunset, my own fatigue, the bitter cold, the clouds. I could never describe it.

Anyway we started down to Lake Helena on the West side. (We'd climbed the Northeast face). The route was across talus, which is more dangerous than scree as the rocks are boulder size. It was the most dynamic slope I've ever been on. I made my move and found myself surfing down on a boulder twice my size. For a moment I thought the whole slope would go. We picked our way along trying to avoid getting pinned under marauding rock.

We looked for a place to bivouac. It was after dark and after a little rock climbing we found a ledge suitable because of a slight overhang above us and its relative stability. Unfortunately it was only about a foot wide. It was 10:10 and had been dark for quite a while. We checked out our new home with flashlights, took off our boots (they restrict the circulation) and sat on them; We then placed the pitons and the slings that would hold us on our little ledge; We used the rope and remaining slings to insulate our backs from the rock. We emptied the packs and put our feet in them, securing loose items in a stuff bag. We put our water bottles between us to keep them from freezing (even then they froze solid). And finally tucked a large poncho around us. The wind blew so hard as to render the poncho not only useless but quite a bother. Our heads and torsos were reasonably warm and protected by parkas as were our feet in our rucksacks; but oh those thighs, with just knickers and long johns between me and that wind.

Contrary to what we thought during that night the morning finally did come. We made our way around and through the saddle pass, and were socked in the face by the morning sun. Not an entirely welcome sight as it made the snow and ice tricky. We collected our animal comforts at basecamp (i.e. the stove, the sleeping bags etc. . .), stuffed expedition packs and went blissfully down the gorge, not without a great deal of self satisfaction.

We went down cross-country (i.e. no trail) and for no particular reason decided to cross the creek at this particular spot. We were down to around six thousand feet and the reeds and foliage were very dense. Bruce caught sight of a red perlon rope—climbers, the first people we'd seen. He thought they were going to climb Williamson, a more accessible peak. About the time I was saying "Look, Herman's knickers." Bruce was saying "Larry's baby blue socks." We looked at each other and decided they were pulling the same sneak job we had so we thought we'd sneak by and let them find our register.

It never occurred to us that they were looking for us, as I had told Mike (who is very reliable) to tell my roommates we'd be home Friday and it was only Tuesday. Unfortunately my roommates had left and didn't get home until Monday afternoon and tied up the phone until Tuesday calling rescue and whatnot.

Fortunately we decided to say hi. They were pretty mad until they found out we'd made the summit. Then jubilation followed. Herman hadn't been too worried as he figured it was impossible to make the summit in less than five days anyway, and with great pride we announced that it took us four, and recounted our trip to Lone Pine as well as our climb, over milkshakes.

We went to Independence to become un-missing persons. As it turned out they didn't send out a search party as they couldn't find the cars (because the sheriff didn't want to take his new Chevy sheriff car up Hogback) and the sheriff hypothesized that we'd gone to Reno . . .

Love Bev

Sorry I worried you.

Mountaineering, like gymnastics and sailing, had its own culture, community, exclusive vocabulary and extended family bonded by shared experiences. Bev was already used to being one of the few, if the only woman in an group of athletic men. The climbing community is also nomadic, a lifestyle Bev had thrived on as a child. The climbers move with the seasons; as abilities and dreams expand so do geographic boundaries. New landscapes are perceived as a challenge and joy, a chance to integrate and strengthen one's identity, rather than as a threat, adversary, or a wasteland to be lost in. The climbing bug was in Bev's veins. In the spring of 1969, with only one semester left before graduation, Bev dropped out of USC and moved back home to Virginia. USC was an expensive school and climbing had changed her priorities. The life of a gym rat was not a far leap to that of a mountaineer.

In the spring of 1969 Beverly began to climb in the Shawangunks, a crag located in upstate New York. She was still practicing gymnastics and was in great shape. In addition to the strength she gained from gymnastics, she was also incredibly flexible, an asset many of the men she climbed with could not claim to have.

San Francisco was not the only place affected by the 1969 summer of love. The Shawangunks climbers practiced their Yoga and had communal crash pads. At the local communal climber's house, Bev met Claude Suhl, who was dropping out, tuning in and doing some climbing as well. They were both involved in other relationships at the time and Bev soon left on a climbing trip out West. But back in Yosemite she and Suhl met up again and completed the climbing trip together. By the time they returned to the East, they were a couple.

Beverly in Yosemite, near Camp 4, circa 1969/70. Photo courtesy of Mike Hoover

While Beverly was with Suhl her climbing began to evolve, although, as Suhl noted in a 1995 interview, becoming committed to climbing was not conscious. He explained:

> Becoming serious about climbing was a decision, but it wasn't one you had to talk about. It was just clear. As in any sport, if you hang around enough you realize that people train at a certain intensity and part of being excellent in a certain sport is having a certain

training regimen. They eat certain food. You see what the the excellent people do, and you hone in on it. You like that certain sport, you want to go to the heights of that sport, so you end up mimicking those who are there.

If you're an art student, you don't just go down to the art museum in your local college, you go to the Met or to the Louvre or something. You want to go with the show.

If climbing was your show, you went to Yosemite for the season, and then you went to the Bugaboos and the Wind Rivers. When you started climbing, that pattern was there for you to see, and if you wanted to get into the big time, you hopped on board the train and you went, there was no need for discussion.

Beverly and Suhl lived and climbed together through that year but by the spring of 1970 their relationship had begun to come apart, and she looked toward landscapes beyond the Shawangunks cliffs.

"There were these climbers who would migrate around the country like a caribou herd, with different herds intermingling," Suhl recalls. In the spring of 1970, Beverly joined the migration, and moved to the Yosemite Valley. As she had said, rocks were where she belonged.

"...Climbing Seems Sane in an Insane World..."

By the year of 1969 people had walked on the moon, young men were been blown to bits by the Tet offense, and America had learned to accept television as a family member that came into their living room every evening with the news, and traded in pedal pushers for bell bottom pants. The speed of cultural change gave people motion sickness.

When Bev—then 23 years of age—moved to Yosemite she became part of a community that had separated itself from the popular culture, and she was partaking in an old climbing community tradition.

A pilgrimage to Yosemite was a rite of passage, an initiation required of all committed climbers. Yosemite was a climbing mecca, the "land of big walls and big climbs," the Oz of a climbing road trip, the center of their Universe and Camp 4.

At one corner of the Yosemite Valley, nestled among granite rocks, giant pine trees, and the Merced River was ground zero for climbers. It was a tent-town with a carnival atmosphere, where the climbers slept, ate, dreamed, bragged, smoked, loved, and dreamed some more. Tom Carter, was a college dropout who had fallen in love with the rock and had become a local resident in this makeshift village of tents and Volkswagen buses. He met Bev there in 1971, and recalls wistfully:

> The lifestyle in Camp 4 was like any commune, with maybe twenty, maximum thirty or forty climbers living in their tents or out of their cars. Everybody knew each other and everybody knew what was going on with each other . . .

Camp 4 was an idyllic basecamp for the ragamuffin crowd of rockclimbers, whose very presence declared their passion for and commitment to climbing. Their love of climbing often seemed more like a physical need. The people in Camp 4 shared a psychological umbilical cord, the bond of an unspoken choice each had made to put climbing foremost in their lives.

In the winter of her first season in the Valley, Bev wrote about her own attachment to climbing. Although people who knew her then say that she spoke often to those she climbed with of how a particular move or section had terrified her and of how being afraid was nothing to be ashamed of amongst climbers, for her parents, Bev focused on the absence of fear while climbing:

> . . . Sometimes climbing seems sane in an insane world. It has a certain element missing from this world. It's a unique environment in which there is an explicit, tangible problem to be solved, success or failure is blatantly obvious, the tools are simple and few and intimately familiar. The solution is always both mental and physical, although failure can result from failure of either. The problem is artificial but the setting is completely natural and subject to the indifferent actions of nature, e.g. you get clobbered by rock fall—and presents its own problems which must be adapted to instead of the usual misguided attempts to do it the other way around. But most of all you can stand on the edge. (Excuse the lecture) An incredible calmness, no panic, no fear—completely controlled but without tension—Really amazing. And besides, the view is just spectacular.

> . . . Gymnastics certainly didn't come easily (as you know) and neither did climbing—the beginnings of my climbing brought dire predictions of doom if I could get that high off the ground. I was told that even if I could learn to climb I'd never be able to do the long Yosemite climbs because I'd never have the strength or endurance to remove pins. (I still can't do a chin-up.) I decided to climb anyway and Tauruses, once determined, are intractable. I just sort of knew, even if I got killed doing it, I had

to do it. Now if I could just transfer all this ego-tripping into some worthwhile channel—Ah! Now to find a worthwhile channel!

. . . if I could only figure out what happened to that $20 I thought I had in my checking account another of life's mysteries would be solved—I'm so full of shit I sometimes find it hard to believe myself.

Love you all — Bev

For the climbers in Camp 4, and for Bev as well, finding a worthwhile channel other than climbing was not a top priority. As Tom Carter tells it in an interview nearly 25 years later, the daily life of a climber didn't hold much else that was a priority at all.

The late sixties were only a couple of years back. The future was bright, people were going with what they did best, and the philosophy was "live for the day." It was like the merry men in Sherwood forest.

You'd wake up and the conversation would go something like this:

"What are you doing today?"

"Well, I was going to go climb *this*."

"Oh, no, you don't want to climb *that!* That's in the shade until one o'clock. Let's do *that*."

And there you went—your plans would change, and on your approach to the route you could change your plans another time, and it would never frustrate you, the lifestyle was definitely *laissez-faire*. Even if you didn't climb, it wasn't a big deal.

If you lived in the Valley, there was always the Merry Pranksters group and then there were those who had a higher climbing level but you were always included and interested in what those guys were doing. Climbing, 5.10, you were still doing early ascents, but everyone that lived in the Valley was climbing 5.10 then. It wasn't the demand, it was the reaching that would be the most fun, how we could find out something in the process. That was probably more of what enthused her, not whether she climbed that route that day or not.

Bev was the first woman in Camp 4 who was truly a climber in that she wasn't just "brought along."

Most women who came to Camp 4 at that time were girlfriends of the male climbers. Besides Bev there were a few other women who had come to climb, Ellie Hawkins, Sibylle Hechtel, Elaine Matthews. Matthews had traveled to the Valley from New York. In 1995, recalling her experiences in the Valley in the early 1970's, Matthews remembers that it was difficult for women to "break into" the crowd of men in Camp 4. She felt her presence was a threat to the male climbers although she differentiated between the really good climbers, who were more welcoming, due to the security they felt in their own talents, she reasoned, and the less established climbers who could make things difficult for her. She said:

Sibylle Hechtel at Camp 4.
Gene Foley photo

> I found it really difficult to find partners. Very often I wound up going out with someone on their day off.

Barbara Cohen, a friend of Beverly's who worked for the park service during this time, recalls that Bev was teased mercilessly by the guys in Camp 4. This was a community whose decisions about what was acceptable were based in the most masculine of definitions. Bev was at times moved to the point of tears by the taunting she received from the guys, about her climbing, or her large muscular calves. In sailing and gymnastics she had often been the lone woman at the front of the field. She was not teased any more than the other climbers teased each other. Insults and taunting were part of the community, to be included in a put-down was to be accepted as a member of the group. For all that the jesting could be difficult to swallow, Bev had spent enough time in similar environments that most likely she understood that the taunting was symbolic of her acceptance, and not to be taken offensively.

Barry Bates, an ambitious young climber from the Bay Area who later became romantically involved with Bev, remembers one joke about Bev that circulated Camp 4.

We had this joke that she was like a draft horse. She had these [Royal] Robbins boots, these big blue climbing boots that made her look as though she had hooves on her feet.

Bev Johnson, Camp 4. (1970)
Gene Foley photo

While Bev's climbing and tenacity were admired and encouraged by the male climbers, she was the one who would have to adjust to the Camp 4 boys' club. For instance Jim Bridwell, a brash young climber who had come to the Valley in the early sixties and was somewhat the Camp 4 guru, recalls:

We'd take girls over to climb on Glacier Point Apron [which is known for its slab and face climbs, not cracks] and I'd tell guys, "Climb over there too much and you'll grow tits. That's where girls climb."

Bev was a *girl*, but since she climbed as well as all any man, she was in a nebulous position. While her gender placed her with the less respected and somewhat outcast *"girls,"* her ability and tenacity earned her a right to stay and climb in the men's world. As the seventies progressed and feminism became a social and political stick of dynamite Bev's position in the climbing community came under more scrutiny. For the most part, however, politics did not travel easily or quickly into the valley.

The free love/turned-on culture of the sixties though, had easily found its way. Drugs were an integral part of most climbers' lives and Bev was no exception. Getting stoned did not interfere with their climbing, as Bridwell remembers:

Climbers were always in a vanguard, but we weren't hippies. We looked like hippies, but climbing was way more important. You'd be walking around the Valley stoned, but you'd be looking at routes.

Beverly wrote home one spring of an accident that turned on more than a few climbers:

> . . . there are helicopters all over this morning. They're salvaging a downed plane from the back country. The small plane was carrying about a ton of marijuana and was ditched, while being chased by the government. Apparently the occupants escaped as there were not any bodies. The plane has been up there most of the winter, providing shelter and comfort for ski tourers, as well as a source of income for climbers and other enterprising folk. Fine article in *New West* entitled, "One Plane Down, Thousands High."

In the Valley, where people drifted in and out with the seasonal tides, relationships were generally open and flexible. As Bev became more well-known for her climbing, her colorful romantic career became part of her celebrity. Dan Asay, with whom she later climbed the *Nose* route on El Capitan recounts:

> All these people get together in like a village and you were villagers. Some guy's girlfriend was your tent mate's girlfriend two weeks before. You all had to accommodate each other's personal affronts or you wouldn't be able to live there . . . We didn't climb exclusively together and for that matter didn't go out exclusively together.
>
> Bev was not a one man woman back then. She played the field. It was part of her aura.

One time Bev was being interviewed by Ken Wilson of *Mountain Magazine*. Her reputation as the best woman climber in Yosemite, and possibly in all of America was growing. They were in the Mountain Room Bar one evening when Ken asked her "How many five ten routes have you led?" She instantly replied, "Well, it's not how many five ten pitches you've led, it's how many five ten leaders you've laid."

Dealing with men was one thing the few women living in Camp 4 had in common. Malinda Chouinard shared a tent with Bev in the early '70s. Malinda was not as committed to climbing as Bev, but she and Bev shared their strategies to lure and to repel the opposite sex. Malinda recalls:

> Bev slept with her climbing rack as her pillow, and her pillow at the door of our tent. Whenever there were scary noises she would reach down and throw a handful of pitons. She said they were good for man or beast.

Bev actually climbed very little with other women. She avoided the all-women's expeditions that were being put together by the Bay Area mountaineer Arlene Blum, although because of her growing reputation Bev was invited to join them. In a community centered around masculine attributes; strength, emotional toughness, the ability to endure, climbing with women could be a sign of weakness. Just as Elaine Matthews had had trouble finding partners, for an aspiring, competitive women like Bev, climbing with another women could be a step down.

She did, however, serve as an inspiration for younger female climbers. Sibylle Hechtel had come to Yosemite in part because she had heard the rumors of an amazing woman named Bev Johnson who was climbing the same routes the top men were. Hechtel explains:

> Climbing all of '69, '70, '71 I never saw another woman climbing once. I had heard of Bev by name long before I met her. It was in '71 and I was in college, and I heard all about this woman in Yosemite who supposedly led 5.9, which was pretty spectacular in those days.
>
> So I picked up everything, drove my car to Yosemite and moved into Camp 4. Beverly was my big hero, she was my idol, I mean a woman who climbed, and led stuff!

Bev wanted to climb and lead it all; smooth faces and jagged cracks, rolling slabs and skin-grating off-widths. Her tenacity in off-widths—routes where the crack is an awkward size that is too large to use jam hands or fingers in but too small to use chimney climbing techniques with one's entire body—was both greatly admired and somewhat disconcerting to most climbers. As Bridwell remembers, her intractability could sometimes be dangerous to her health:

> She's the only person I know who's climbed the left side of *Moby Dick*, in shorts. It's one of those smooth, leaning flared chimneys. Afterwards her knees just looked like someone had taken a cheese grater to them.

Despite her accomplishments, expectations of Bev's ability were still defined by her gender. As he tells it, Bridwell and his climbing partners would use Beverly as a way to determine the difficulty grade of their climb. While 5.10 was the standard of the day, when Bridwell and his friends would climb with Bev they'd know the grade of the climb because, "if she could do it, it must be only 5.9," he recalls.

On the other hand, being a woman made Bev more accessible to some of the climbers in Camp 4. Tom Carter reasons;

> Because she was a woman it was easier time bonding with her than with the guys who would look at you sideways and judge you more on your ability than your enthusiasm.
>
> Bev was just a fountain, latching onto anyone's enthusiasm. It was great climbing with her because it was always like exploring. She didn't care to know too much information about the climb, she'd say "Oh, this sounds like a neat place to go, there's a couple of climbs there."
>
> Other people were more detail intensive about the climbs, or what equipment they required. She just wanted to go climbing and go to different places in the Valley. That's what Valley climbing does for you, it gets you up off the valley floor.
>
> She'd just say "Oh, this is girl climbing." Which meant it required good balance or was difficult to read, and not just something you grabbed and pulled on.

Bev and Bridwell spoke of *"girl climbing"* with different tones, hers of explanation, his of rejection, but they both were describing the same kind of rock, and despite their differences, Bridwell and Bev were close friends. During her first season in the Valley Bridwell became Bev's mentor. In addition to being a fantastic climber and a Camp 4 fixture, Bridwell was quite a *"Don Juan"* and soon the two were dating as well.

That winter Bev migrated up to Tahoe with Bridwell and several other climbers who worked seasonally for the ski patrol. To support herself she set up a small sewing business making down jackets and packs and selling them to the ski patrol. Her make-shift factory was downstairs in the cabin she lived in and each time she would emerge from her work a cloud of feathers would announce her arrival.

Bev had never learned to alpine ski and so Bridwell got her a pair of 207 team skis from the French ski team and some cut-down skipoles. She was given some boots from the sister of a friend. Bev was about 5'5" and one hundred-twenty-five pounds.

Mike Hoover photo

At 207 centimeters, the skis were far too long for her. But Bridwell left Bev to fend for herself and when she wasn't sewing she would tromp off and practice. Occasionally she would see Bridwell or other friends on the ski patrol and they would give her a few tips. One day, while skiing down one of the most difficult runs on the mountain Bridwell recalls, he was astonished to find himself barely able to catch up with a graceful skier, who surprisingly turned out to Bev.

She wrote to her parents that winter:

Hi Folks -

Can't decide whether or not I like skiing downhill. I love cross-country because it's so free (in all senses.) But this chair-lift, slide down I can't decide about—For sure it isn't destined to become a life passion of mine. Managed to get a pass one day—Rode the chair up, skied down, rode the chair up again, watched the ski patrol dragging the wounded off the field - skied down, rode the chair up, froze, skied down. Why, why, why do people pay $10 a day, to say nothing of clothes and equipment for that? Can't figure it out.

Some people must not like money very much. Nobody who has ever gone skiing will ever be able to point out to me the complete pointlessness and absurdity of climbing without getting laughed at. What a way to get your jollies.

I was about to write off skiing altogether when I discovered skiing fast—must be what's getting everybody off—It's certainly what's getting them racked up. All those nice carved turns must get boring pretty quick—so off they go—bunch of speed freaks.

Skiing's OK and I'll certainly go anytime I get a free pass. It just lacks something—Can't pin it down—Maybe it's because I haven't had to work for it. I haven't had to bleed. It's the first thing that's come naturally to me. I can just do it, and each time I get noticeably (at least to me anyway) better . . . .

Bev put most of her energy into cross-country skiing. Those were the days of wooden skis and Bev's pragmatic motto was "Judge your equipment by how easy it is be to repair in the field." Tom Carter who skied with Bev frequently remembers that she once used a tree to scrape the extra wax off her skis rather than giving up because she lacked a proper ski scraping tool.

Beverly and Bridwell broke up that Winter, but returning to the Yosemite Valley in the Spring, Beverly began dating the climber Barry Bates.

One of the first routes Beverly and Bates climbed together was the *Crack of Doom*, which was then rated as 5.10a. On their return to Camp 4 Bridwell and Galen Rowell—another established climbing pioneer—greeted them with more than a little skepticism. Bates recalls:

In the campsite we were staying in, Bridwell was there, and Galen Rowell happened to be up for the weekend. I think he was staying in our campsite. He asked me what I'd done that day, and at that point *Crack of Doom* probably had only a half dozen ascents.

He looked at me, and I was this 20 year old whippersnapper kid as far as he was concerned. He said "No, you didn't do that . . ." And

I replied "Yeah Galen, that's what I did today." So I finally convinced him that I had done it, and he asked, "Well, who'd you do it with?" I pointed to Beverly and at that point I don't think he said anything, he just kind of shook his head.

Bev had already climbed Half Dome and the north face of Sentinel Rock before she started climbing with Bates. Together they did the first ascents of *Lunatic Fringe*, *Five and Dime*, and *Vanishing Point*, all of which are rated as difficult 5.10s today. Back then they were some of the most difficult routes being done.

Most climbers lead climbs of a lower difficulty than those they follow because of the additional threat of a leader fall and the difficulty of placing protection, but Bev was able to consistently lead climbs at the limit of her ability.

Althoug following was no easy task, Bates explains the situation in the 1970s:

> I think following those routes was in some respects physically harder than leading them, because we were still climbing with pitons and you had to hang there and actually pound things back and forth to get them out. It was demanding, just physically, to hang there and get the stuff out.

When Jim Donini, a tall gaunt man who had been introduced to climbing through the Green Berets, met Bev in the Valley late in 1970 she was already a fixture there with the nickname, "5.10 Bev." He knew her reputation for being tough.

> . . . Five of us went on a crack climb. Beverly was desperately ill that day and even though everyone said, "If you don't feel good, Bev" . . . but she was bound and determined to climb. I had led the pitch and went up over this overhang and Bev was second. She got up below me and I could hear her getting ill, barfing everywhere and then she came up, a big smile on her face, of course. The other guys had to climb through her mess.

Once Bev went to climb the east buttress of Middle Cathedral Rock. The approach is through boulders and on the way up she slipped and twisted her ankle. It swelled up but she laced up her boot and climbed the entire route. Afterwards she went to the Valley doctors and was diagnosed with a fractured ankle.

After another incident she wrote home:

> . . . I broke my baby toe in a bizarre accident. The bizarre part being that I don't remember doing it but it now articulates sideways at a right angle. The cure is to wear sandals for four weeks, which, with three feet of snow, is a bizarre treatment indeed.

Bev's pain tolerance and sheer determination became part of her legend. Tom Carter reasons:

> I never saw her freak out. One day another climber and I were hanging out in front of the local pizza joint when Bev came by after having just finished climbing *JoJo*, a hard 5.10 finger crack. Bev had led the climb but had sacrificed all the skin on the backs of her hands to do it. The backs of her hands were solid scabs and my friend sucked in his breath and pointed in awe and amazement as Bev came by.
>
> She was the first woman to command the respect of the men in a male dominated kingdom, I don't think she intended to do that. I just think she wanted to do what it happened to be all these guys were doing. She didn't have plans in her life, at that time, she wasn't embarking on this program to be the best female climber in the world, all that stuff was just sort of a pleasant side effect. She just wanted to climb.

Mike Hoover photo

Another time during the winter Bev was carrying a pack full of food and first aid gear out to a support station on a cross-country ski race. Skiing out there, she noticed how uncomfortable her pack was. She tried to adjust it while she was skiing but never stopped to take her pack off. When she arrived at the support station and removed her pack she saw that her knitting needle had punctured the pack's fabric and almost an inch had been lodged in her flesh.

One evening Beverly and Barry Bates decided to sleep above the Cookie Cliff formation at the west end of the Valley rather than in Camp 4. Bates recounts:

> It was almost dawn when I was awakened by scream, and I was just about to say "Did you have a bad dream?" when I looked over and saw blood on her shoulder and there was this bear standing right there!
>
> I got up and chased the bear off with a stick, and what we figured happened was that she woke up and the bear was actually standing on her and had his nose two inches from hers and she screamed at that point, and then it bit her. At first we both thought she'd been clawed, but looking closer it turned out she'd been bit.
>
> It was a fairly young bear, probably a couple hundred pounds. It was a black bear, though I think it was more curious than anything else. She was a little freaked out, but it was that pain threshold thing I remember.
>
> We drove down to the clinic. She would panick and freak out about stuff when she was on the ground. When we got off the ground, while climbing, everything was Okay.

✳✳✳

For one day at least in 1973, when Beverly went to climb the *Nose* on El Capitan with Dan Asay, everything even off the ground was far from calm and stable. Dan Asay had first met Bev in 1970. He was walking along the base of El Capitan looking for new routes, and heard a tirade of profanity coming from above. He looked up, only to see a woman leading a difficult crack climb, and figured it had to be the amazing female climber

Beverly Johnson whom he'd heard so much about. She saw him, stopped swearing, for the moment, and smiled. Soon after the two were to become good friends, climbing partners, and briefly lovers.

Bev approached Asay after failing at an attempt to ascend of the *Nose* with her friend Donna Pritchard, one of the few other women climbers in the Valley. Though she and Donna had been frustrated by their slow pace and difficulties hauling, Bev wanted to finish the climb, and convinced Asay to go complete the route with her If they succeeded it would be the first time the route had been done with a woman swinging leads. Elaine Matthews had done all but the last day's climbing several years before, but she and her partner had been stormed off the final pitches and had agreed to a somewhat unnecessary rescue.

Asay and Beverly were also bombarded, but not by weather The story of their climb became part of the legend surrounding Bev. As with any legend the story was sculpted and reformed as it was passed on from climber to climber The current version is that on the second day of climbing Bev was on the lead. Hearing noise from above, she looked up and saw what she thought to be a haul bag plummeting towards her As it passed by her she realized it was an unfortunate human being. The climber fell past her and landed with a resounding and terminal thud at the base of El Cap. Bev turned to her partner, "Well, you don't see THAT every day," she said, and proceeded on her lead.

This version of Bev's reaction added to the flavor and character of her image, but the real story reveals more of her sensitivity. While Asay enjoys hearing the revised version of events, he recalls well what actually happened that day:

> Bev had just led the pendulum in the Stove Legs crack, on that first pitch. I was just starting to follow it, lowering off from Dolt Tower I heard some shouting. I looked up, saw this trash falling down, and figured someone's dropped their haul bag and yelled, because there were a couple of parties ahead of us. One was a group of Mexicans at right about the Great Roof, and there was a party right near the top.

It was coming down right at us, so I kept my eye on it and I saw it take the form of a person, and it flew past not too far away. Thankfully he disappeared out of sight just before hitting a ledge below. It made an awful sound, he was obviously dead. He looked like one of these dummies they throw off a bridge in cheap movies.

I was already focused on following this pendulum. But Bev was just sitting there, and she yelled at me, "Did you see that?" in a kind of quavering voice. I said, "Yeah I did," and continued climbing.

I got up there, and she was pretty upset. We thought about going down for a few minutes, but decided we couldn't do that because we'd end up rappelling right down where he hit, so we decided to go up. She was very concerned that we'd come across his partner splattered on a ledge above.

Otherwise the climb went on like clockwork. Although we were swinging leads, she got the crux leads and the route was no problem for her at all.

It took us five days. At the top, I'd had it. I'd thought it was a vertical backpack trip. But she was glowing like was the best adventure of her life. And soon after that she and Sibylle Hechtel did the first women's ascent on *Triple Direct*.

✻ ✻ ✻

Charlie Porter, whom Bev dated from 1972 to 1975, wrote in 1994, about rappelling to meet Asay and Bev, during that climb.

> She had done the *Nose* on El Cap with Dan Asay. I was quite jealous and . . . maybe I did what I did in an effort to impress Beverly . . . I don't know. I rappelled down from Camp VI and spent the night with them. I took old ropes and rappelled half the way down just to see her. It was a crazy thing to do.

Porter was an eccentric man who did most of his climbing alone, and had revolutionized big wall solo climbing. His technique and climbing methods began a new chapter on the history of Yosemite big wall climbing. He and Beverly were both close friends, and lovers.

I first met Bev in Yosemite the same weekend as they were landing on the moon. When I saw her again in 1972 we got together, and were together until 1975.

She told me she took up with me because I had been married, and she felt it would prevent us from getting involved. Well, that didn't work.

We didn't do too many walls together, though I did a lot during that time. She was always at the base waiting for me, shouting up. I think she had to work, and she had fire fighting and ski school. But we did a lot of free climbs, at the end of each day we'd go climbing.

I would always be soloing, and she would show up at the base and watch. I had taught myself to climb, so soloing came naturally to me, and I encouraged her. She wanted to learn to do aid climbing alone on big walls, so I taught her my system. When you do solo climbing like that by yourself you have to really concentrate, you can't lose your concentration. She got right into it; she could enjoy and understand it.

When she was on the way up to solo Washington Column she was at odds on whether she would do it or not. I think it is because I carried her stuff up there with her. It felt funny to both of us for me just to turn around and leave. But finally I did just leave her there and she did quite well. In the end it was a good moment. Then she got right into it. She used my exact same system.

That summer Walter Rosenthal and I got interested in doing an alternative route to the *Nose*. Maybe Bev and I were having trouble then, I don't remember. But we were looking at a long angled climb on El Cap, that I was going to call *El Cappidosia*. Bev was sitting in her hammock belaying and reading a book about a perverted football player and his perverted fraternity initiation involving a backwards race and the loser eating grapes. The route was so contrived we decided to use the scene from that awful book to name the climb the *Grape Race*.

During a long hooking traverse around the corner, in the usual wind, I could hear her cry, "Charlie, Charlie," but she couldn't hear me answer. It was like she thought I'd left her or something. She was almost crying but I couldn't make her hear me, so finally I broke all the rules and just completely untied and climbed back to her to show her I was OK. But she pulled herself together and started swinging leads. She had been on a lot of big walls recently. Maybe it was a little bit of a nervous break down, or maybe too many days on the walls.

That night we had a lovely romantic night, on Camp 4 ledge, completely relaxed.

Then the next day we looked out across that expanse of unbolted granite we needed to traverse to stay on our route. I looked across at the corner and it was a bit contrived. It didn't go as I had hoped it would and we would have had to go back to me bolting and her belaying to finish. And she'd been on El Cap for so long, it would have meant more sitting around.

Our route hit the *Nose* at the point above El Cap Towers. We would have had to traverse over to bolt a completely blank wall, with lots of hooking. In those days it was a real first to do something so contrived. I was the only person doing that type of climbing at that time, so really we wouldn't have been swinging leads there.

So we just made the decision to bag it and go straight up the *Nose*. It was mainly just because we wanted to go fast again, to feel the climbing, nice and fast.

And we did too; we made really good time for that long ago. We did the upper pitches in the dark. I really wanted to do that climb. I had planned it for so long. I had some regrets later when Walter Rosenthal came back and did the finish, but not really.

Beverly understood you can be living on a big rock face, and enjoy it . . . It takes a day or two to get into it and then it could be forever.

"KEEP UP THE PAYMENTS ON MY LIFE INSURANCE..."

Coming down from *The Grape Race* with Charlie Porter after so recently completing the *Nose* with Asay, and the *Triple Direct* with Hechtel, Bev was drained emotionally and physically.

October 18th, 1973

Dear Folks,

Hi. Writing you on the occasion of my giving up climbing for the 400th time. I've gotten too paranoid and it doesn't seem worth the risks.

Got down yesterday from another seven day bout out on El Cap, this time a new route with Charlie. It was an interesting experience although the wall was rather blank and devoid of ledges, so all functions had to be performed while suspended and there was always the worry of dropping some crucial item and being stuck in the middle of El Cap without it.

I was still fairly strung out from the *Triple Direct* which I had finished five days before. My mind was still boggled and my wounds still open—an incredible set of blisters from my boots, chunk of meat still missing from my hands, my back raw from my waist loop. I couldn't believe I was going back up. Extended climbs are at least as punishing mentally. Can't relax. Seven days of trusting life to flimsy gadgets and fragile ropes. Got to stay alert. No mistakes—Ran out of food and water and had to sprint for the summit, climbing most of the final night by headlamp and moonlight.

Walkout eight miles the next morning. Very tired but glad to be released from the clutches of El Captain at last. Walking through the forest along the rim. The forest and the wall seem surreal by turns. It is impossible to hold them in the mind together. Ethereal forest. Cool autumn shade for parched throat. Slender white aspen with yellow leaves, gold grasses, dark conifers. Down a thousand switchbacks, feet protesting. Endless switchbacks. Finally Camp 4, home free. Yogurt, beer, two hours in Roger Rudolph's bath tub, and 20 minutes cleaning the same.

. . . too late for Pete Thompson's wedding, although the mopping up operations still going on at the reception—lots of drunk climbers and Rangers are still there. Tim Harrison was killed that morning with some other fellows. It doesn't sink in. I'm too tired. I'll think about it later. I see his face in my mind over and over. But I don't feel anything. Nobody seems too upset, which seems strange. There are a few people in tears, I sense the rage against death in others, many are drunk from the wedding. The accident is discussed, and there is intellectualization on the shortcomings of equipment, puzzlement over the fatal gadget. Tim had contributed to his own end, had used it wrong, but now . . . hadn't we all.

Off to Pete's to wish him well. Incidentally I have met all sorts of Aunts and Uncles, Moms and Dads.

The world has changed. Gerald Ford (Who's he?) is on the cover of this magazine. The Jihad is in full swing in the Middle East. I feel like I've been to Mars.

Must be time to do something else (if there was one other thing I could do, God, just one other thing.)

Start working around Thanksgiving which isn't too far off. looking forward to skiing and going to Europe in the Spring if I can save enough money. Do you still want to go to Spain mom? I ought to start looking into tickets, passport etc . . . . Can't hang around here in the Spring, I'd only lose my resolve and start climbing again.

Love to all of you. Very tired.

Good night.

Beverly

For Beverly and the other climbers of Camp-4 death, mortality, pain, and loss were part of the life they had chosen to live. For some it was part of what was so compelling about hard climbing, the knowledge that the decision you made on the rock really did have life or death consequences.

Tim Harrison. Doug Robinson photo.

The choices defined your life and often the lives of those you cared for. The saying that mountaineers "conquer" the mountains they climb describes the internal struggle to face the fear of death, to make a choice to risk themselves—and others—rather than the battle against any outside force. This can be seen as morbid, or life-affirming. Most climbers would say they feel it is the latter, and for many—Bev most likely among them—the higher ante are both enticing and a dark shadow to the motivation for climbing, to feel life intensely rather than flirt with death.

Many climbers learned to face death, and made some money working with the Search and Rescue, or fire crew teams that operated in the Valley. Bev joined both, and though she had proved her abilities on the rock she had to face some antiquated attitudes before she was accepted in the Search and Rescue community.

To prove her mettle to one fire crew boss she was asked to move several big boulders around. Once a member of a fire crew walked off the job when he heard that he was going to be working with a woman crew member. In reality the fire crew was an ideal job for Bev. Her stamina meant she could carry the heavy packs for miles on end and she knew the Yosemite terrain intimately.

Beverly herself understood, that to some degree, her fire crew boss' doubts were justified. The expectation that she would be weaker than a man, was based in reality, and she told journalist David Robert's for an article *OUTSIDE* magazine in June of 1981:

> I'm sort of an anti feminist. I do think women are weaker. People make such a big deal out of making people the same. But I know what I can lift and what my boyfriend can lift. If you have to pick a fire crew, for example, out of a mass of people, you would pick the guys first. If not only for cultural reasons— you'd have a better chance of getting somebody who'd used a shovel before—but also because they're bigger and stronger.

This reality though, did not interfere with her attempts to do the job. Sure she would admit that the scale she would be judged by was a masculine one, but that didn't mean she couldn't do pretty well even on those terms. As with gymnastics and sailing, and growing up in a household with a father in the military, the measurement of ability and worth by masculine values and attributes, was what Bev understood.

Beverly rarely had the chance to climb with women partners, but one of the few close women friends Bev had was another National Park Service employee, Donna Pritchard. The two women were known for the marathon cross-country ski trips they took together. They were also occasional climbing partners. In the fall of 1973 Bev and Donna had made the first attempt at an all-women's ascent of El Cap, an ascent which they had to abandon. Although Donna was as passionate a cross-country skier as Bev, she was not as accomplished a climber. After reaching Sickle Ledge, Bev and Donna realized they were not up to the hauling the route would require. They hadn't planned on enough climbing days and had packed their bags too heavily, and chose to retreat. They left the haul bag up on Sickle Ledge. Bev retrieved the bag on the ascent she made soon afterwards with Dan Asay.

In March 1974 Bev and Donna went on a six day ski tour with three other women, which turned out to be more frustration than pleasure. At that point, Bev had been invited to join a all women team being assembled by Arlene Blum to climb the Annapurna, and she was considering the offer. She wrote about the trip:

Six days with five women is sure a drag. Makes me wonder if I want to go to Annapurna, at least on an all women's climb. Donna Pritchard and I ended up with most of the community gear on our backs, and doing the trail breaking (an arduous task in wet snow) which would never happen with proper men along. Anyway I began to feel like a combination pack animal and guide as I know Donna did.

The weather was wretched, necessitating vigilance and para- noia. Route problems generated by the increased avalanche possibilities; in addition everything was wet, going to bed in a cold soggy sleeping bag, getting up colder and more tired than I went to bed, trudging through the snow, discomfort and paranoia; the slab sinks and fractures three feet above me, quickly cau- tiously skiing in reverse, don't slide, don't slide. We back off, go around the slope, way around—through the trees up and down— finally we get to Lower Ottoway Lake, conditions on the pass make it out of the question.

Donna and I went off to explore the upper basin. The clouds came in and Donna's colors were barely visible ahead. We were very very paranoid, careful to stay on the rock rib. The snow slopes now had the aspect of a tumultuous sea. In the end how- ever we managed to replace fear with prudence and took turns spotting each other from relatively sheltered points.

Coming down from the basin was outrageous, the only possi- ble justification for the risk and the bother. The light was so flat that it was impossible to judge the terrain, it had to be felt, fast too. Quite a bit faster than I would have gone had there been some way to control my speed . . . . Oh well, I can't describe this sort of thing. It's one of those, "you know" experiences. Either you have plunged through a cloud in a desolate basin in a

Sierra winter, white air, white earth, or you have not. It does not relate or compare to anything else.

I took an amazing crash, where the slope dropped away. All Donna saw was flying powder and my avalanche cord and she thought I'd gone down in a slide, when I was only tumbling along head first. This resulted in a bent ski which was satisfactorily straightened later between two trees.

Anyway that's all the adventures we had. One stupendous ski run and five days of utter drudgery . . . .

Beverly would decline Arlene Blum's invitation.

Bev first met Mike Graber, a climber from the east side of the Sierras who had made his reputation climbing new routes in Alaska, on a rescue in 1974, her reputation preceded her. Graber recounts:

I met Beverly . . . actually . . . everybody *knew* of Beverly, if you climbed, you knew who she was. She was in magazines and back then it was "Wow, this woman climbs 5.10!" She was really famous and very attractive. I was seventeen years old, a few years younger than she, . . . anybody would have had a crush on her!

I went up to climb the south face of Watkins with Rick Ridgeway, and another friend, Rob Muir, in the fall of '74.

The approach was slab climbing but then it got into these ledges where you criss-cross back and forth.

You had to go to the highest point, and then stand up on this manzanita bush to reach a mantel, and then mantle up. Rick's about 5'4" and Rob Muir and myself are both around 6 foot. For most people it was a scary third class move, but since Rick is really short, he had to go higher up on the manzanita. He also had these one gallon water bottles clipped to hardware loops around his shoulders and they were impeding him from getting close to the hold. As he went higher up on the manzanita, the plant broke, he pitched off backwards in the air. It looked like a sixty-foot fall, it was probably only twenty five, but it was a long long way.

We were up above and watched him pitch off, headed for this lower ledge, and I knew, he was either going to splat on the ledge and get killed right there, or he was going to tumble off, and go tombstone-locomotive to the bottom. He landed on the ledge on top of his water bottles and the water bottles just exploded, cushioning the blow to the body. The only injury he sustained was he just broken EVERYTHING in his ankle, all the bones, it was just pudding.

Rick Ridgeway.
Photo courtesy of Mike Hoover

We went down and managed to get Rick to the bottom of the slab and on the ground. Then Rob Muir ran to the Valley.

Four hours later Beverly shows up. She heard that there was a problem, and ran in and got there hours before the next rescue guys. She just burned in there, got Rick all comfortable and everything, and then left, probably at ten at night or something, because a helicopter was due in in the morning. When she knew everything was under control, she said "Well, I'm going to go back to the Valley." We were all astonished, "Wow, who is that woman?!" Of course everyone knew it was Beverly Johnson.

When the rest of the rescue guys get there, we said, "OK, everything's under control."

That was how I met Beverly for the first time. The legend of Beverly Johnson I was familiar with, but I met the flesh and bones Beverly Johnson on this rescue. In some ways that rescue characterized the rest of our relationship. It seemed that in the years that followed there were countless times when she was bailing me out. Not literally a rescue, but figuratively. She was always helping me out in some way or another.

Graber and Bev did climb together after Bev left Yosemite, but in 1974 her plans did not stretch that far. At that time she was more concerned with making her money stretch to the next meal. Once she and several other climbers were on a rescue mission on El Cap. While they were waiting to be told the rescue plan, they entertained themselves by climbing on a boulder on a traverse near Thanksgiving ledge. Even though they were waiting, they were all being paid and Bev dubbed the boulder problem "the twenty-seven cents traverse" in honor of how much they earned during the time it took them to traverse the boulder.

Rescues were dirty and tiring operations without much time for fun and games. Bev wrote to her parents about a particularly frustrating expedition:

> When you had called we had just returned from a foray into the hinterlands of the Bridalveil Creek drainage to rescue some stranded explorers. We found them at 3:30 am after an exciting night of trudging up the avalanche debris in the Spires gully on NPS snowshoes that were self-destructing, and postholing down the other side through and sometimes on top of giant snow-covered manzanita bushes during a wonderfully wet snowstorm.
>
> By the time we arrived our victims were in better shape than we were, having fallen (literally) into a small but fine cave. We pitched the tent in the only convenient spot which was on top of a snow covered manzanita. The tent collapsed twice by small avalanches and eventually we gave up trying to sleep and came back to the Valley after a few more misadventures.
>
> Excellent way to earn a living? Keep up the payments on my life insurance. — Bev

Beverly covered her basic needs with her patchwork of jobs; ski instructor, Search and Rescue and Fire crews, and sewing rescue gear and equipment for the Park service and friends. In her jobs for the Park service she wrote, ". . . I'm still plodding along, which is the only speed I ever move (This has been mistaken by calmness under pressure from my supervisors.)" But her sewing offered her respite from the rigors of Park Service work and some time for herself.

She made packs and sleeping bags and contracted with the Park Service to make parkas. By 1974 she had bought a good sewing machine and set up a little factory alongside Charlie Porter's foundry work in a building in

Briceburg, just west down the Merced River from the Valley itself. She wrote, "I really love my factory. It's the only place I'm alone for long stretches of time and can sit and build things. I'm always quite contented when I work there."

She considered launching a serious business with it but wasn't motivated to deal with the financial end. Meanwhile her commitments with the Park Service were growing, though in fits and spurts:

> Am going to helicopter school on my next day off to learn about the capacities of the Navy helicopters, etc.
>
> It should be pretty interesting. Lt. Commander Morse has great style (or maybe he's just a flaming ass hole. Pardon). He once volunteered to lower us to Heart Ledge (on El Cap) on a cable. We demurred—"The top's just fine, Thanks!"
>
> Helicopters make me nervous. I had to jump out of a hovering one once on Sentinel Rock as the top was too small to land—on. Hopping out on a point of rock 1000' above the Valley did in my nervous system. Getting in again wasn't much fun either.

She added later:

> The new news is that I went to get checked out on our end of Navy helicopters today and it became arranged for a couple of us to go through their helicopter training program for two weeks at the beginning of April . . . . At any rate I doubt that the CO will like that action too much, so I'll probably be replaced.
>
> Oh well, think of it, our family's third generation of Naval aviation shot down by male chauvinism. I can hardly consider it a crushing blow since I've walked out eight pretty unpleasant miles rather than ride in a helicopter. And today didn't exactly bolster my confidence. They didn't bring the cable and the hoist . . . had trouble with the cable breaking. There's no back up so there's food for thought when you're being picked up by cable . . . .

While work had its ups and downs, life in the Valley continued to flow smoothly and for the time being Bev was happy to float along. Adventures off the rock included a spring swim across the length of Tenaya Lake in her bra and panties which she told Dan Asay was her "cold hardiness conditioning." Ron Kauk, who had been smitten with the climbing bug and at 16 came and moved to the Valley spent many days climbing with Bev. Their routine consisted of climbing in the sun then stripping down to swim in the Merced river. Responsibility beyond the day's or even hour's events was not a weight to bear. The goal was simply to continue living that day.

However much Bev wanted this golden time to continue though, the world beyond Yosemite began insidiously creeping in. As the years passed, she began to reflect more often on whether her lifestyle was becoming stagnant. She wrote:

> I have a job for sure with the Park this summer. Found that out today and that's quite a relief, although being a climbing ranger isn't suitable life's work either. But what is? I don't know . . . .
>
> Ah, alas, things will work out somehow. I'm happy for now. And I can't think of what I'd rather be, given what I am, except more orderly. So I deserve what I get and hope it's not a prophetic remark.
>
> Goodbye, write. I'm in line for free dinner so I got to get.
> — Bev

For the time being at least, the future was secondary to dinner.

"I STAND FORKED BY THE ROADS..."

In the spring of 1974, at age 27, Beverly's restlessness got the better of her and the serenity of the past years began to waver. Her climbing had given her great notoriety, but within the limited scope of the outdoors world. She made a modest living with her sewing, ski instruction and rescue work, none of which she had great ambitions for. She had an itch but was not sure where to scratch. There were several roads for her to take, and each held adventure, but the costs and the rewards of each were, for the moment, equally illuminated. There was nothing to push her firmly down one road over another. The options were clear, the decisions were not. Though she claimed to be content, her very contentment irked her.

1974 March

Ho Hmmm. Sitting here trying to decide the course of my life, or at least that portion over which I can exercise some control. Many possibilities loom ahead. I stand forked by the roads:

A) I can go to Alaska and maybe get killed trying to climb the Moose's Tooth, Or I can just go there and ski around and stay out of crevasses (I'm becoming a chicken in my old age.) This is very cheap - $400 for 2 months. Plus a crack at one of the finest (and unclimbed) faces around.

B) I can go to Europe . . . climb in the Alps or sit at the seashore, visit museums?—Could learn German, work, etc.—Broaden my views. What does one do in Europe anyway?

C) I can go to Russia, or I can go to Nepal next spring

D) If I could afford it I could do a, b, c

If I wanted to I could afford it.

The problem is that it's much easier to do nothing—I could have money in the bank, or soy beans for that matter. I could pay back my good parents—I could be a climbing guide in Yosemite another year, another year as a ski instructor. I enjoy it. It supports me short term. Ah yes, the ugly question, what next? I am utterly contented. I wish I were 27 forever, that Yosemite would always be the same. What a bore I am. I kick myself. Smug complacency. Surely with the entire world there are other things to do. I would like to go back to school but what would I study? I would like to love someone but am afraid to cast about in that sea. I would like to have children in my world but not in the larger one. What sort of hopes could they have?

Have just babbled myself out of paper. So it's off to the mailbox. — Beverly

That summer Beverly's climbing became less focused as well. She wrote to her parents admitting that, "The drive for climbing comes and goes—corresponding to my attachment to my life and my skin. My attachment to my hide must be at a new high because I sure can't climb."

Being unable to find the motivation to climb may have come in part from the tragedy she was dealing with on the ground.

Donna Pritchard had been injured in a car accident that left her confined to a wheelchair. Bev became Donna's primary caretaker. She commuted from Yosemite to Reno where Donna was hospitalized initially and then later to Fresno where Donna was later moved. One of their bonds as friends had been to share the strength and stamina each had in their outdoors pursuits. Bev understood the extra pressures the loss of this part of Donna's identity put on Donna. Bev wrote:

The thing that's hardest to put up with is people's optimism. Donna's so tough, everybody just expects her to get better. What they fail to appreciate is that this isn't a matter of will. It's hard on Donna as she doesn't want to disappoint anyone.

Donna returned to the Valley in her wheelchair. Bev helped her to make the adjustment but was also firm about not indulging Donna in any self-pity.

Dan Asay noticed that despite the care and attention Bev showed Donna, when Donna, "needed a bit of a kick in the ass . . . Bev was the one to give it to her."

Bev spent most of her time attending for Donna, helping her to find ways to enjoy the Valley. Donna was able to work for the park service again at the visitor center. Together she and Bev would go tearing around the Valley floor, Bev wearing her roller-skis as she pushed Donna in her non-electric wheelchair. This worked great except for the occasional hair raising descent. Donna also became practiced at emptying her catheter on various Ranger's patrol cars.

However, over time Donna's spirits deflated and she fell into deep depressions. She became suicidal and attempted to kill herself several times. Bev tried to buoy Donna's attitude but at some point was only able to witness helplessly as her friend's desire to live faded away.

Finally Donna received the settlement from her insurance company. With the money, she left the country for a trip around the world, taking an attendant with her. She died while she was in Asia, from a broken spirit as much as a broken body.

Watching Donna's slow disintegration invited questions about Bev's own future and the fragility of her lifestyle and where she would be if that were taken away from her. Donna's losing battle forced to the surface the issues about the direction of her life that until now Bev had left to simmer. She wrote in September of 1977:

> I was offered the job of running the ski school at Elk-horn/Sun Valley. I don't have much enthusiasm for it, but there are some incidentals like money that make it rather appealing—though it seems yet another extension of this rather easy life that I am none too excited about, though the opportunity to ski every day is hard to pass up. I am weary of resort life, resort folks, but city life is as yet untenable—must be time to homestead on the Yukon.

Homesteading however, was to take a back seat to the health insurance and income Bev found in the increasing interest Hollywood showed in climbing.

"I'VE NEVER REGRETTED NOT LEARNING TO TYPE..."

A few years earlier Bev had begun getting jobs acting, small parts or stand-ins, or doing stunt work for the various commercials and TV shows which were increasingly coming to Yosemite. As the biggest female name in climbing, Bev was often the first name mentioned when a woman who could climb was needed. She was left cold by the fanfare surrounding the filming operations but was grateful for the tangible rewards of the work such as money and health insurance through the Screen Actor's Guild.

Hollywood's descent upon the Valley for a production provided climbers with experiences that were in sharp contrast with their ordinary hand to mouth existence. Climbers were often hired as riggers or extra labor. Their crew status allowed them access to the extravagant buffets and facilities each production brought along.

Bev was amazed at the luxury and the lunacy surrounding the film crews.

March 4, 1974

. . . The film crew is here and that's quite a circus—what an entourage! Hair dressers, wardrobe folks, make-up, portable dressing rooms with flush toilets, cameramen, electricians, gaffers and grips, all manner of assistant directors, and assistant producers, the whole incredible array.

My part got cut . . . so I was transformed into the fluffy little wife of the Star Ranger, Matt Harper, and am summarily chopped in the first 50 seconds of the show, bumming poor Matt out for the duration (Great plot huh?)

I was paid $600 for my death plunge. Although I was later told I could have gotten a lot more, that's still a bunch of money—Couldn't get into the movie business—too much standing around.

Have been doing the alterations for the costumes for the movie. I've never regretted not learning to type and I'm wishing I didn't know how to sew.

Miss you all — Beverly

Bev found some harmless humor in the Hollywood maelstrom but other Valley locals reacted to the the film crews as an enemy invasion. These protesters were incensed by the film crews' disregard for the environment. The activists, led by Charlie Porter (who was dating Bev at the time), used their climbing skills and creativity to sabotage the filming. Charlie Porter describes the elaborate lengths he and others went to undermine the productions:

Dan Asay and I monkey wrenched the climb the night before, by putting thousands of beer cans and stuff in all the dicey moves to make it impossible for them to climb it. When they were going to do an off width crack, we wet it down, [making it too slippery to climb] Dan and I nailed *Bishop's Balcony*, filling the crack to spoil the commercial.

When the series *Sierra* came to the Valley, Bev got right into it. I did it only because she did. In reality, I worked against Universal Studios. When we found out where they were going to be the next day we would go out and soap the cliff [again, making the rock too slippery to ascend.]

When she went to work in the morning with hundreds of people, [the climbers] wouldn't be able to climb because we had taken bar soap and rubbed the handholds. They would have to send for fire engines to wash it down. She would know it was us, but she wouldn't tell. She was quite proud but also loved the work.

They sent some thugs to try and get rid of us. The rangers tried to get rid of us for soaping the cliffs. The thugs slashed tires and blamed us, but all Bev's friends and I were doing was soaking cliffs, and sending in photos of it to the Sierra Club. I was doing this with her climbing buddies, not her.

They spray painted the Rostrum to make it match the rock where they had been filming before because it had too dark lichen. They also spray painted Tuolumne meadows. We took videos. It came out against commercialization of the park, and half the folks quit after the bad master plan came in showing there were more commercial plans. We did that lots of times. It took us seven or so months to run them out. Their last day we were throwing dirt clods at them. When they found they were canceled the head actor took the microphone and called up, "You win, Charlie."

Bev worked for the film, did big stunt falls for the show, and did rigging, getting cameras organized. It was some of the first industrial rigging. Bev would say that for a park that has public transportation and paving, doing something like this would not make it any worse.

She was proud of being a member of the Screen Actor's Guild. She was interested in making a good living and knew it wouldn't be cross-country skiing. She was supportive of what I was doing but she was making good money, and her career took off from there.

During the filming of *Sierra* Bev began to date the lead actor, Jim Richardson. Through his work on the series in the Valley, Richardson had become interested in climbing.

One day Richardson partnered up for a climb with Mike Hoover. Hoover stood 6'4" with a broad chest, thick brooding eyebrows and searing dark eyes. His reputation was even more imposing than his physical presence. He was a film maker known for both his brilliant cinematography and the militant perfectionism which he demanded first from himself and then from all those around him. In his drive to create his films he could be variously suave and charming and brash and confrontational. His temper had a hair trigger and brutal edges which were felt by all those closest to him.

Hoover remembers that on that day, in their decisions about where and what to climb, he took Richardson's declarations of advanced climbing skills at face value. It was not until the actor was on the lead, struggling on a climb clearly beyond his ability that Hoover realized the mistake he had made in taking Jim on his word. Unable to help beyond belaying, Hoover could only watch as Jim peeled off the rock and plummeted to the ground.

Bev arrived at the hospital to find Richardson in critical condition with near fatal injuries and Mike Hoover standing sheepishly nearby. In Bev's mind the accident had been Mike's fault. The ownous was on Hoover, as the more experienced partner to judge Richardson's abilities, despite all the inflated claims, and take the movie actor on a more appropriate climb. Bev let Hoover know how she felt by simply refusing to acknowledge his presence.

Bev's opinion of Hoover had been far from positive even before this event. The first time Bev had met Hoover was in the Yosemite Valley when they were near each other on the same climbing route. She was climbing up and he was rappelling down. At the beginning of rappelling one pitch Hoover threw the rope over the edge without yelling the requisite "rope!" warning to those below. His rope landed on Bev and her party. As she climbed up and past Hoover coming down, she swore up a storm, cussing him out for his incompetence. Faced with a pissed-off Bev in mid-climb, Hoover, as he tells it now, was struck dumb, and completely smitten.

Hoover had also received some mixed reviews from Bev's circle of climbing friends with the production of *Solo*, a short action film which he had made in Yosemite and which later won him an Academy Award nomination. Though the film was well received by reviewers, the climbing community had a different opinion. The beautifully shot film detailed one man's solo rock climb. Many climbers felt that in allowing the general public to witness the nirvana of their climbing world, Hoover had betrayed their select and proudly isolated society.

Mike Hoover had become involved in both climbing and film making through his love of birds. As a boy he climbed cliffs in order to follow the birds he was fascinated by. He began taking still photos of the birds and then transitioned to moving pictures as a way to capture their flight. Hoover relocated frequently during his childhood, as his father, a businessman, changed jobs and moved around, and like Beverly he found that this developed his ability to adapt to new environments. Dropping out after one year of medical school he honed his cinematographer skills making pornographic films, until he wedded his outdoorsman skills with his film making and camera knowledge. He filmed and directed the TV series, *Survival of the Fittest,* which pitted adventure athletes, climbers, kayakers, runners etc. against each other in grueling outdoor tests of endurance and strength. He quickly gained a reputation for his outdoor adventure films. Mike had been married twice and had two young children, Erik and Holly.

At the end of that summer, and through the fall, Bev worked on a Columbia Studios series, *Steadman,* about, as she put it, "an Olympic ski racer who comes home to be sheriff." Segments of the film were to be directed by Mike Hoover.

Mike Graber was also on the *Steadman* shoot, working as a rigger and cameramen. Hoover had heard of Graber's pioneering climbs in Alaska and was planning to use Graber in some upcoming expeditions, but Graber needed more training behind the camera. It did not take long for the two men to strike a friendship. As Graber's congenial attitude worked well as a balance to Hoover's brooding antagonism.

Bev had not been easily convinced to work with Hoover and arrived on the shoot with Hoover still firmly on her blacklist. But it was on that shoot that her resistance began to crumble. Hoover remembers the course of events leading up to their reconciliation:

> I was the second unit director on *Steadman,* which means I directed all of the outdoors stuff.
>
> The show involved a bunch of outward bound type kids, and a leader, getting stuck on the side of a cliff, where the leader falls and is killed, and the kids fend for themselves. One of the parts called for a girl to step forward and be pretty bold and heroic, taking over after this guy is killed, and at that point there were really very few girls to choose from that could do it. The one that always came to mind of course was Beverly Johnson, she'd be the best.
>
> So a friend of mine, Rick Ridgeway, was working as production coordinator, and I said, "Why don't you see if we can get Beverly to work on this, you'll just handle it, she won't even have to talk to me and I won't even talk with her, we won't even talk with each other."
>
> "Yeah, I might be able to do that," he said.
>
> So he called her up and she said, "Oh yeah that's great, that is good," until he mentioned my name, and she went, "Oh, no way, I don't want any part of it, forget it."

But I knew she was in the Screen Actor's Guild and that she would be hungry for the work so she could keep her health insurance.

So I told Rick, "Tell her she doesn't have to talk to me, she doesn't even have to see me. She will just be off doing something and we will film her from a distance, and it will be fine."

"OK," she agreed.

So we went to Elephant's Perch, this real neat giant rock near Ketchum, Idaho. We went in there with all doubles . . . with Beverly . . . doubling somebody else who's going to do all the close up talking which we don't have anything to do with.

It started to snow. . . . and the next day it snowed all day, the real wet miserable kind. We had a big big big big fire, and I had a poncho and I was standing by the fire. Beverly came out of the tent and up to the fire. She didn't see who was standing around, she just came to stand by the fire.

It started snowing heavier, and she leaned up back against me without knowing it was me, and she said "Do you mind?" She pulled part of the poncho over her, but then she looked up and saw it was me and she was kind of in shock, but she didn't want to lose her cool so she just stayed there. That was kind of the turning point.

After we finished shooting, I had to stay to do some more filming, and I had the only motel room left there. She had to make some calls. I said, "You can use the phone in my room."

She stayed there waiting there for the people while I was watching the World Series. She ended up falling asleep on the bed.

I pulled the covers up over her and took her glasses off. She woke up there the next morning, and that's how we slowly became friends. It was a very slow melt.

At the point when her relations with Mike were thawing, Bev had a full plate of opportunities and diversions. She had the chance to go to the Arctic with Ned Gillette, a skier, climber, and sometime boyfriend, who had received financing for an expedition to Ellesmere Island, in the Canadian Northwest Territories off the northwest coast of Greenland. Her hesitation was, as she wrote to her parents, "Polar bears eat about one geologist a year, and I have no interest in being the annual geologist."

She also had another option, "to raft the Amazon [sic] and get eaten by piranhas." This was an option that included being with Hoover. Bev would be a climber on an expedition led by Rick Ridgeway to climb a volcano called Autana in the Amazonas province of Venezuela. Hoover and a camera crew would be filming the trip as a television documentary. For Bev, it came down to death by chomp or nibble. Nibbling won out, influenced in part by the fact that she had re-injured her arm and felt it was too weak for Ellesmere.

Undoubtedly another reason why Bev chose to go to Autana was her changing relationship with Hoover. After the initial breakthrough Bev had continued to warm up to him. This was to some extent the result of a little deviousness on his part. A jubilant Hoover remembers:

> After filming up there maybe a few months later for the same series, Bev had to go to Salt Lake to catch a plane. I was driving back to Jackson, Wyoming (which really isn't that close to Salt Lake City), but I said, "I will drive you down to Salt Lake." During the drive I just kept asking her questions, and she was talking away, and I drove straight to Jackson instead of to Salt Lake.
>
> When I came down Teton Pass she said "What did you do?!"
>
> I said, "I kidnaped you!"
>
> She didn't complain, and so I took her to my place in Jackson. I thought she would like it, but she really didn't. Later on, same exact place, you couldn't get her to leave. So I don't know if she was pretending she didn't like it or really didn't.

Beverly and Hoover found that, despite their differences, on many levels they were kindred spirits. From music to literature to politics their attitudes and interests were the same. Their relationship grew fast from that point on. Soon they were living together and Bev's life, which until this point had meandered along now gained speed and direction. Together they were driven and determined, with styles that covered a spectrum from *gentele* to crass and combined and created a momentum to be reckoned with.

"...THIS THING ABOUT EATING PRIMATES"

Autana, or *"The Eye of the Gods"* was a giant dead volcano in Venezuela at the top of which was a large cave. From the ground this cave appeared as a dark, eye-like orifice, hence the name. The expedition team included both climbers—Beverly Johnson, Mike Graber, Jim Donini, and Rick Ridgeway—and the film crew, Mike Hoover who was the head cameraman, director and producer, and two other cameramen, Peter Pilafian and Don Burgess.

The team's goal was to climb the volcano as they would a big wall in Yosemite, explore the cave, and then continue climbing to the summit, filming their adventure for a documentary they would edit together after they returned.

Jim Donini. Michael Graber Photo

The original concept for the Autana project came from Rick Ridgeway. After watching many of his climbing friends market their mountaineering skills in the television and film business, Ridgeway decided to follow suit. He approached Hoover who told him that before he could make a climbing film, he had to have a concept, an idea or story, that he could find a network to subsidize. Ridgeway came up with the Autana climb, and Hoover agreed to make it happen.

Having Beverly on the team added to the marketability of the piece by breaking up what Graber called, the "climbing film formula," which he describes:

. . . the boys get together, they go camping in the woods, they see pollution, shed a tear, climb the mountain and go home. Bev was the perfect person to have along to break that. In 1977, God, almost 20 years ago, a woman climbing up through spiders and shit . . . .

Also, Bev was comfortable being the only women on the expedition. Graber recognized that Beverly maintained her balance between being a woman, and being one of the guys on the crew, by navigating some of the double standards he admits he and the other men held:

If you have one woman with a group of guys and she has to pee. Some women are very candid about it, 'I gotta pee, you guys do it right here, I'm gonna do it right here.' But among guys that's kinda brazen.

Everyone expects, a guy has to take a pee, he just whips it out and takes a leak right here. But the girl does the same thing, she just squats anywhere, then she has no decency. It doesn't matter that the guys do it.

But in my experience of climbing with women, Beverly seemed to have an additional element of dignity, to very modestly position a pack, or step around an ice block, even though you're all roped together. Which in my estimation is a very nice trait, because it's not easy to do.

Maintaining boundaries of any sort was a challenge on a intensive expedition. However, one reason Bev may have done well climbing with all men was that she was able to also make clear when she felt they had gone too far. Graber again:

It's not easy if you're with guys all the time. Hoover and myself, and Ridgeway, we talk about all sorts of things. When it got a little too explicit sexually or into the gutter, sex talk that guys do on trips, she would say something as simple as 'Oh, you guys, can't you have anything better to talk about?' But from Beverly that would be like as if she was shouting obscenities, proclaiming her disapproval, from the top of her lungs.

To get to the jungle area that led to the base of the climb the team had to first travel by boat along four different rivers: the Orinoco, the Sipapo, the Auntana, and finally a tributary of the Auntana, the Manteo. The logistics of moving the entire team down river proved to be a Catch-22. The team was carrying all their climbing gear as well as the film equipment. The heavier the boats got, however, the more likely they were to run aground if the river wasn't deep enough. If they overloaded the boats then they would be leaving gear like a Hansel and Gretel trail along the way. The outcome was that the group was chose to cut back on food.

After navigating the rivers the the group had to trek some twenty miles to the base of the climb, through a triple canopied jungle. This meant that looking up offered the same view as lying face down in a giant fern. The heat was also intense and they had to carry gear for the climb as well as the film production. Periodically they would stop, and one person would climb a tree in order to break through one or two canopies, to determine their position in relation to the cliff. They knew they were at the base of the climb only when the vegetation suddenly went vertical.

The climbing itself was awkward, dirty, and sometimes ridiculous. At times, unable to even reach through to the rock, they simply climbed up the massive foliage that covered the entire cliff, vertically bushwhacking. Bev, at one point forced to complete a difficult move by pulling up on an unsteady root, joked in a clip that made it to the final film cut, that her "life was hanging by a limb."

Bev, Hoover and Donini separate gears at the end of the expedition, on the Amazon Basin. Michael Graber photo.

During the climb the food supply became seriously low, and persistent hunger pushed everyone to the limit. Over the course of the trip each climber lost approximately twenty pounds. Tolerance and humor were threadbare as everyone reached varying degrees of clinical insanity. The food they did have often succumbed to the jungle before they could use it. Graber winces at the memory:

We were starving, it was pretty brutal. We had this big can of sugar. Flies had gotten in the sugar and laid eggs, because sugar holds moisture and every time you opened the can up it was just full of flies. So you had to sift through the sugar. For anybody that's a fairly stressful situation.

And there's Bev, just even keel.

Mike Hoover photo.

While everyone else was going loony Bev seemed to be able to maintain some stability. Whether she was simply great at masking her emotions or she was able to push her hunger aside and not let it affect her, Bev's ability to maintain her serenity certainly benefited the group.

However, in light of the food shortage, one slight gag they had brought along in the hopes of getting it on film backfired. They had brought from

America a gag can of peanut brittle, the kind where a wire coil snake shoots out when you open the top, with the idea of filming the reaction of whoever opened it. Not everyone knew about the can and one of those still in the dark was Jim Donini, the ex-green beret. By this point everyone was subsisting on small amounts of tuna fish, and larvae infested sugar

A frustrated Jim Donini kept asking what was with the peanut brittle. He was told to wait until they reached the top. Finally, after reaching the giant cave, two thirds of the way to the summit, Donini grabbed the peanut brittle and announced he was going to divide it into equal portions. Unfortunately Donini was standing on the edge of the cliff when he made his proclamation. Those in the know tried to persuade him to come away from the edge but they were talking to a hungry, tired, pissed and stubborn man and before they could convince him, the cap was off and the snake flying. Donini did not fall off the cliff but, Graber says, "He looked around with bonfires in his eyes, for someone to kill." No one cracked the meekest grin and a death silence echoed through the cave chamber, until, with a resounding "FUUUCK . . . ." Donni tossed the can over the edge.

The food shortage continued to provide some of the trip's most memorable moments. The expedition was supported by native guides who helped the group to navigate through the jungle. The native's support, though well intentioned, was sometimes gruesome. Even Bev's tolerance proved to have limits. Donini recounts:

> The Indians would catch tarantulas and bring them over to show them to Beverly, and she'd try and be polite but she wasn't into it.
>
> We were filming up there in these caves, about 17 pitches up. We were there for a couple or three days, and we ran out of everything, as I recall all we had was Celestial Seasonings tea. (Now I don't have Birkenstocks and I do real coffee, so I was not too happy about that.)
>
> Anyway we get back down to camp and basecamp was about a mile from the mountain. Then it was about six more miles out to the river where our Indian guides had a camp set up. We had to wait several days for our boats to come in but the Indian guides had

eaten all of our food down at the camp. So we said, "Hey, this is a cornucopia, go out and get us some food from the jungle."

They went out hunting with this old shotgun and came back with these two small monkeys. They skinned the monkeys and threw them into this big pot to boil. As I recall they gutted them but left the heads on.

One little monkey was on top of the other, and you could see the back of his head and shoulders sticking out of the water as it bubbled along. We were all sitting there and Beverly was looking at this scene, and I could tell she was not happy.

They decide to serve these monkeys and got a big fork, stabbed one and started pulling it out of the water. But Beverly started protesting that it wasn't done, "No no put them back . . . ."

They looked at her, put them back in and boiled it some more. Then they brought the monkey out again and this time she was protesting again, but they ignored her. We were all sitting on a log and Beverly was sitting right next to me as they came up to each person and put some monkey meat on their plate.

They got to Beverly's plate, and this Indian took the monkey's forearm, cut it off at the elbow and placed this arm with hand and all on Beverly's plate. . . .

I glanced towards Bev, and she met my eyes. She looked at the plate containing the monkey limb, looked around, took a very tentative little bite of it, threw it down, and went running back into the woods. She was pretty brave, and I guess she felt like she had to try it.

Finally she came back and sat down. She was very embarrassed by not being able to eat this monkey, her face was ashen, white, and she looked at me trying to explain and said, "Jim, I, . . .I just have this thing about eating primates."

I looked right at her and said, "Oh, Bev, I never knew that was a problem of yours."

On top of the gastronomical adventures, surviving the climbing, the heat, and terrain, the team had to make the film that was the final objective of their journey. Even with the most sparse film crew there were thousands of dollars in camera and sound equipment to worry about, sound and lighting factors to keep in mind, not to mention having something interesting happen to capture on film in the first place. A regular film production in an enclosed studio is a big undertaking. Hoover had built his reputation on the fact that he could pull of a film production on a cliff, in a jungle, "hanging by a limb."

To do this he had to envision the idea story line before the filming began. With a fiction film the crew works off a script. Each day is designed according to what the script calls for. A documentary film maker does not have a script to guide him, but most often he has some story line or envisioned sequence of events. The trick is then to go with the flow as life inevitable rearranges that story-line several times over.

> I remember—Donini recounted—when Hoover said, this is going to be a "ficumentary, and if anything weird happens to you guys during the day, don't tell anybody about it, because I want to get it on film that evening, and I want to get the right expression, so that no one knows about it."

> One day Rick Ridgeway says, "Something happened to me," and Hoover says, "OK, don't tell anybody." We gathered around that night on this ledge with a lantern going, and we were supposed to be telling about what happened that day. Ridgeway continues telling his story: "I'm climbing, and I pull up on this hold and I reach up and GOD, there's a tarantula there, eight inches from my face!'"

> "God!," I yelled, and a shiver goes down my spine . . . .

> Immediately Hoover screams, "Cut Cut! Goddamn it Rick, we are supposed to be the best climbers in the world and you're going to tell the world that you're afraid of spiders?"

> Ridgeway thought that he had a good little thing but Hoover, as director, thought it wouldn't fly. So it was scripted, but we actually did it.

In addition to the peanut brittle the team brought along a rubber snake for a scene conceived in the U.S. In the end the snake scene proved to be the high point of the film. The scene begins with Graber climbing up to a ledge. He reaches out to grab a hold then recoils in fright, screaming. He whips out a hammer attached to his belt and begins to pound on something on the ledge. Ridgeway, belaying Graber from below, is heard yelling up, asking urgently if Graber is OK. Finally after a few "just to make sure" swings, Graber maneuvers what appears to be a large and now very dead snake onto the handle of his hammer and passes the snake over slowly in front of the camera until he has twisted around backwards with the snake dangling over the jungle abyss below, into which he drops its lifeless corpse. The villainous serpent is dead and our beloved hero can continue his journey.

Later this scene almost got Hoover into deep water. Chuckling, Graber tells what happened:

> We came back to the States, the film's shipped off to ABC. The Network loved it, and they call in Hoover, up to the fifteenth floor or whatever, where they are showing the film, and they ask, "Mike, what kind of snake is that?"
>
> "I don't know, it's just a snake." Mike Hoover answered.
>
> "Well, we've got to find out what kind of snake, was it poisonous?" And he says, "I don't know what kind of snake it was"
>
> "Well, don't worry," they reassured him, "because we've brought in the reptile expert from the Bronx zoo to look at it."
>
> Then they freeze the frame and blow it up like fifteen feet by thirteen feet on the wall.
>
> The expert from the Bronx zoo comes up with a magnifying glass, while Hoover is sitting in the back with beads of sweat pouring down. He told me it was blown up so big you can almost see *Made In Taiwan* on its stomach.
>
> The zoo guy studies it, and then concludes that while he's not sure if it is poisonous or not, but it is definitely a new species.

What Hoover understood was that in order to sell, documentaries had to have gripping story lines. He could shoot as much beautiful footage as he wanted, but in the end it there wasn't some story to keep the audience watching, then the footage, beautiful or not, was wasted. The networks knew this too and depended on an engaging story to sell the ad spots throughout the time the show would air Unlike a feature film where you can control the highs and lows, in a documentary you have to use what happens and what is around you to create story.

In the late 1970's selling documentaries was much harder than it is today with so many cable channels eager for good shows. Graber articulates the difficulties they faced back then:

> The only way you could sell then was if the show delivered somehow. If you had some kind of excitement in it, if it was a linear storyline that people could follow: The boys want to climb this but there is this problem and this problem, OK, but suddenly they pull together and then you have a nice story and the public can follow that, but more importantly, you can sell 30 second ad spots around it.
>
> If you became known as having documentaries that never had peaks of excitement, never had resolution, never developed a story, you were out. Because you were only as good as your last film. So there was a tremendous amount of pressure on adventure film makers to deliver really high octane goods.
>
> Hoover could do it, because he was willing to tweak, he was willing to make ficumentaries rather than documentaries. Whereas a lot of other guys, it was *cinema verite*. "We only shoot what happens."
>
> In his mind, if you don't have a story, if you can't keep an audience to your film, then what good is the film, no one sees it anyway. You can use your craft to mix elements and build a story, so you have a beginning and an end and you resolve the dilemmas, and keep the audience interested on your story.
>
> Hoover wanted entertainment. To his credit he knew more about television back then, than television knew about television, it's entertainment.

Cinema verite is almost impossible on a climbing film. If you filmed the climb as it happened it would be all butt shots, not great entertainment. Simply depicting accurately on film the angles of the cliffs and the climbers' position can be a logistical and technical circus. Climbing is best shot from above and to the side so that the angle of the climb is clearly depicted on the screen. The final scene in the Autana piece is a panoramic shot of the summit of the volcano, which was taken from a helicopter. It depicts the incredible view and landscape from the top as well as capturing the majesty of the Venezuelan jungle and the towering volcano. So in tweaking reality, using perspectives that technically none of the climbers could have had from their climbing position, the cameramen created drama and produced emotional feeling that would be better understood by the viewers. Documentary? Docudrama? Does it matter? These were questions Hoover and Beverly would have to answer for themselves, and more often justify to others, again and again.

Incongruous as they may appear the lifestyles of climbers and filmmakers actually dovetail smoothly. Both demand dedication, focus, odd and exhausting hours. Both offer new and interesting perspectives on the world that require creativity stamina, an eye for detail to discover. There are times when both a long climb and an intricate production are like a house of cards, the integrity and strength of the whole dependent on a variety of delicate connections. Each provides a tangible sense of accomplishment and a threat of failure. Each are as distant as can be from the life of eight-hour days and two weeks of vacation a year.

Upon their return from Venezuela, Hoover busied himself shooting the *Survival of the Fittest* for ABC and Bev took off for Yosemite to work on a project that had frustrated her for years—a solo climb of El Capitan.

"PEOPLE EITHER UNDERSTAND OR THEY DON'T WHY YOU WOULD SOLO A BIG WALL I DON'T THINK YOU CAN REALLY EXPLAIN IT ...I CAN'T"

As you enter Yosemite Valley driving down highway-120 El Capitan dominates the view, its presence a summation of the mystery, legend and magnitude of Yosemite. The scale of El Cap requires an acknowledgment of the larger forces at work in the universe. Bev was never an arrogant climber. She had wanted to solo El Cap because it was a personal challenge, an internal yardstick she measured herself against. Bev's brother Ted once said of her, "Part of a lack of confidence is a fear of failure, and Bev didn't have that fear. If she couldn't do it, so what? Would she try? Sure." She had failed at several other El Cap solo attempts, beaten back by weather or bad planning. This time she felt prepared for every eventuality, but understood there were no guarantees. She gathered her gear and on October 17th, 1978, she began to climb.

The climb itself generally went smoothly, but on the Valley floor, despite the fact that Bev had alerted only a few people to her plans, a storm of publicity was brewing. Beverly's friend, park ranger John Dill, was as surprised as other park locals at the magnitude of public interest Bev's climb stirred up. The October 28 issue of the *San Francisco Chronicle* quoted him as saying that he only gradually realized that "to the general public Bev's climb had great dramatic appeal. The first woman to do it, and in this age of the Equal Rights Amendment and all." Beverly was a beautiful young woman exploring a harsh and spectacular landscape in a time when women pioneers were being celebrated—all this added up to a story with an angle irresistible to the media. Reports of Bev's progress made it to the nightly news and the climb received a deluge of press coverage in the Bay Area and national newsmedia.

The main focus of attention was certainly Bev's gender. This held a certain irony for Bev, who later told a *Times* reporter,

> . . . the feminist movement doesn't rate much attention among
> the mountaineering subculture. We generally think of ourselves as
> girls, not as Big Women. We're not feminists because we're not
> forced to be. The men don't polarize us. They treat us as climbers
> with certain strengths and limitations, and they help us as equals.

When a very tired but smiling Beverly reached the summit she was greeted by a fleet of reporters and cameras. She seemed to enjoy the hoopla and publicity. She mentioned to one reporter that she did not mind the company, because it meant she wouldn't have to carry her haul bag all the way back down to the Valley. But Dan Asay commented, "I think she would have been just as happy if nobody had been there, she could just sit on a boulder and gloat over what she had done."

Bev was invited to appear on the television game show *To Tell the Truth*, and on *The Johnny Carson Show.* They played "Climb Every Mountain" as she walked on stage. When Carson asked her, "Why do you do it?" Beverly shrugged and replied, "I have no idea."

The publicity Bev's El Cap climb received catapulted her name recognition into an arena where she had the ability to generate attention and thus sponsorship for the upcoming adventures she had planned with Hoover. Their immediate schedule included filming an all-women's excursion through the jungles of Irian Jaya in New Guinea, via visit to a native tribe of former cannibals, and their first trip to Antarctica.

The Antarctica expedition was intended to be the realization of a dream Mike had held for a long time—to sail down to the Antarctic, winter over, dogsled to a peak, climb it and then do a live broadcast from the summit.

This is a real dream for Mike, Bev explained in an profile for the *Los Angeles Times* July of 1978, For me it's just what I want to do now.

In June of 1981 David Roberts reported in *Outside* magazine:
Her El Cap solo was probably the finest climbing feat ever performed by an American woman. But Johnson publicized it not at all, not even with an article in a mountaineering journal.

I'm not very articulate. I have a kind of mission, with the films, to introduce people to cannibals or tell them a little bit about Antarctica. El Cap didn't have any of those features about it. It was just me. People either understand or they don't why you would solo a big wall. I don't think you can really explain it. I can't.

Though Bev's opportunities for travel and adventure opened up after her solo ascent, her explanation of her motivation to climb never wavered. She said, "I climbed El Cap for the same reason I climbed all the others. I love to climb."

"...the Last Wild Place"

After El Cap, Bev was consumed with the preparations for Antarctica. Hoover was unable to get the funding to do the entire project as he had originally envisioned it, so they devised a scaled-down version.

Before they left, Beverly made this entry in her journal:

> When I was a child my father had a lot of maps. Some had large blank areas. My father said they used to put pictures of elephants or dragons in them to cover up the their ignorance, but now they simply put "No relief data available."
>
> I was sorry that the dragons and elephants were gone but the maps with "no relief data available" were always compelling. When I ordered maps for our Antarctic trip, I was pleased that there were great gaps in the map series. "Maps unavailable," the letter informed me; some of the maps which cost $4 each were completely blank except for a small comment, "No significant geographical features," so they would not be sent back as defective.
>
> It was as good as if the maps indicated it must be the last wild place. It is.

Later Beverly wrote in her journal what appears to be a rough-draft of a sponsorship letter. It documents her fascination with Antarctica.

Antarctica Assets Unfrozen.

The fact that the Antarctica continent belongs to no one is hardly surprising. It is the coldest, highest, driest and most inaccessible region on earth. Until now it has been protected by its very uselessness to man. On the surface it is not much more than 5.7 million cubic miles of ice. But the story is below the surface.

The U.S. proposed a treaty "designed to preserve the continent of Antarctica as an international laboratory for scientific research and ensure that it be used only for peaceful purposes." The International Antarctic Treaty was signed in Washington on December 1st, 1959 for an initial period of thirty years starting June 23rd, 1961.

. . . much of the environment history is locked in the Antarctica's under 9,000 vertical feet of ice. Note gyrocopter in photo. Mike Hoover Photo.

This treaty for the first time in history devotes a large area of the world to peaceful purposes. It is the first treaty which prohibits nuclear explosions unconditionally. The treaty provides for open inspection of all bases. It is the first treaty to provide freedom of scientific investigation over large areas . . . . The Treaty is often referred to as the 'model' for international co-operation and a 'blueprint' for environmental protection.

The value of Antarctica's vast natural laboratory is unique. Free of its own industrial and urban pollution and remote from the centers of civilization, . . . much of the environmental history of the planet earth is locked in Antarctica's 9,000 vertical feet of ice.

The story is beneath the surface.

Because of the economic and political consequences resulting from any significant discovery of minerals, it was quickly recognized that any attempt to legislate for this eventuality would undermine the entire Treaty. This "undermining" legislation (for mineral exploration) was passed June 2nd, 1988.

Every nation conducting research in the Antarctic has become involved in the quest for the region's mineral resources, some overtly, but most covertly.

The story is beneath the surface.

The Antarctic has provided a model for international cooperation. However, the treaty is beginning to split apart along national lines as mineral exploitation has become feasible. There can be no justification for the exploitation of Antarctica except in terms of human greed. Should we be bend to short sighted national greed which will postpone the day that we start to deal with the problems of finite resources? Should we do it at the expense of the earth's last wild place? Whatever man does to the web of life, he does to himself. When the smell of man is the only smell, it will be the end of living and the beginning of survival.

NOTES: The question that is being asked in the Antarctic is should we be retreating to nationalism at a time and in a place that should be looking forward to a new ecumenism that is the best hope for the future of the planet?

Beverly told David Roberts for *Outside* that her biggest hopes for filming in the Antarctic were to increase awareness of the precious wilderness there. But in the midst of preparations for the expedition, decisions focused on how much pasta to bring rather than how to save the environment. The expedition team was made up of Hoover, Bev, Mike Graber, and Rick Ridgeway. Unlike the Autana expedition, this team was a self-contained unit with each member responsible for both climbing and technical filming activities. There was to be no separation between camera crew and talent. The expense to simply get to Antarctica was so large and the budget so tight that the four team men would have to work as the talent, film crew, sound crew and repair whatever broke in the harsh Antarctic conditions. Bev had already become proficient at working the sound equipment and to some extent the cameras. Graber and Ridgeway had filming responsibilities as well. But Hoover was the indisputable "general," the leader and director.

The preparations for the trip were intricate and immense. The food for the entire trip had to be sorted and organized, the personal gear included the special skis and sleds each member would use to move on the ice. Bev wrote her parents a postcard on May 20, 1978:

> Mike and I have been busy trying to procure dogs etc . . .
> It's a headache to get them and that's just the beginning, since
> their favorite activity next to pulling sleds is fighting.

The greatest frustrations came with attempts to gain support from the National Science Foundation which could grant official access to Antarctica for Americans. Hoover, however, was unable to get the director's approval for their expedition and so the team was left with no choice but to book passage on a tourist liner and essentially jump ship once they reached Antarctica.

The first leg of their trip though, required flying to Argentina to meet the boat. Bev packed her carry-on luggage full of the densest items such as the lithium batteries and raw film. Her carry-on backpack could weight up to sixty pounds. Graber cringes:

> The last thing you ever wanted to have to pick up was Beverly's
> carry-on. And you never even wanted to be sitting underneath it on
> an airplane, stuffed above, because the plane crashes, and you'd be
> crushed by Beverly's carry-on.

Traveling through Argentina, as an attractive American female, Bev would often have the Latin American men at the hotels or the airport trying to carry her bags for her. She would usually say, "No, thank you," but often they would persist. Finally, to appease them she would consent, only to receive looks of amazement, dismay and chagrin when the men were barely able to lift her packs off the floor.

The team had booked passage to Antarctica on the cruise ship, the *World Discoverer.* The ship resembled a floating rest home as the other passengers were generally men and women in their seventies who could afford the close to 20 thousand dollar passage. The team of climbers stood out like a dirt smudge on white linen, especially when they appeared at dinners in T-shirts when the other passengers came in suits, ties and gowns. The expedition members bought one way tickets, but were unsure if they would be allowed to get off the boat in Antarctica. They were able to talk their way off the ship by convincing the captain that a British Antarctic Survey boat had agreed to give them a ride back. In reality the British captain had told them he would give them a ride but that he had no definite schedule as his progress was dependent on the ice conditions. So although they were allowed off the first ship, there were no guarantees they could get a boat back home.

Once off the *World Discoverer* they used two inflatable, rubber boats with outboard motors to get to the shore where they would begin their trek. Zodiacs have four separate pontoons which make them especially good for ice travel. If one pontoon is punctured there are still three left inflated.

Michael Graber and Beverly maneuvering one of the inflatables into position.
Mike Hoover photo.

Arriving on the ice was the beginning of the adventure. There had been few if any private expeditions to Antarctica in the last thirty years and the team had a sense of real exploration. For Bev this trip began a love affair with the frozen continent that motivated her to make over seven trips to the Antarctic in the next 15 years. The white expanse and the freedom that came with the isolation of being in "the earth's last wild place" started to resonate within her and never stopped.

Traveling on the continent was an arduous process. All expedition members wore special skis and hauled a sled behind them stocked with climbing gear, supplies and film equipment. They were able to reach their destination, an area called "The Forbidden Plateau," without serious incident and once there summited a beautiful but unstable peak. While climbing they had to be careful that each hold they grabbed did not come off in their hand, or worse, fall onto the climber below.

For Bev this was also chance to continue learning the technical aspects of filmmaking. When she had first met Hoover her experience in films was limited mainly to work in front of the camera, stunt work and bit parts. To work on the adventure films Hoover made however, she needed to know how to operate all the camera and sound equipment. Hoover had originally hoped that Bev would spend more time in front of the camera on the films they worked on, but Bev shied away from that and focused instead on perfecting her technical skills.

For her this had nothing to do with defying gender roles. On the contrary, for the Antarctic film she wore a wig with long braids that stuck out from under her thick wool hat and and on film her wig was the only physical distinction that made it clear she was a woman, as they were all bundled up like Michelin men from head to toe.

The trek to the peak and the climb itself took longer than the group had planned and left them little time to return to the coast to meet their boat home. They had to push full speed to make it back to the seacoast before the last boats to South America left for the season. Unfortunately, they had only the vaguest idea when exactly the boats would be leaving. Arriving at the shoreline they had to re-inflate the Zodiacs they had left there and race out to the point where they hoped to catch a boat. Graber details their wild ride:

> One of Hoover's favotire stories about me is we were coming back from the Forbidden Plateau and we were in a rubber boat and we see a boat in the distance, the the liner *Bransfield*. We thought

that was our only chance out of there. But in rubber boats in high seas, the wind wants to get underneath the boat and flip it.

So we burn off with the engines wide open, dodging ice because we think this boat is leaving and it's headed out to this strait of water, the Gerlache Strait, where we knew it was going to be big sea and real dangerous in the Zodiacs.

We pull up next to them, waving, they wouldn't stop. Of course they could not hear us.

There was one guy on watch, he looked over, and we were the last people in the world he expected to see, these people in these rubber boats.

But they turn into the wind and come to a stop. We pull up along side.

Do you have any beer..? Mike Hoover photo.

All the passengers went down to the rail, and looked down at these four people in these little rubber boats. There was this embarrassing silence. What we want to do is ask them if we could have a ride back to South America, and we didn't want to let the last boat out of Antarctica leave, so I decide to brake the ice by asking; "Do you have any beer?"

There was this silence up on the rail, and they looked at each other, and then they burst out laughing.

"Yeah, we got some Scottish rubbish we can't stomach."

It turned out that this wasn't the last boat to leave, and Beverly, Hoover, Graber and Ridgeway were able to get a ride with an Argentine boat instead, as well as keep their case of Scottish beer.

"...IT'S LIKE YOUR FOOT —YOU MAY NOT LIKE IT AS YA GET OLDER, BUT YOU'RE KINDA ATTACHED"

When asked about her future plans in a November of 1978 interview with the *Los Angeles Times*, Beverly said, "I'm on short time now. I want to have children, a family—it's kind of like Thoreau leaving Walden Pond—I could go on climbing forever, but it's time for other things." By 1979 Bev had not left her metaphorical Walden Pond, and was adventuring more than ever. But she did take a step towards her plans when, on October 14th, she and Hoover decided to get married. This would be Mike's third marriage, and for Bev it was a decision that meant a change from her earlier attitude towards romantic commitment. She was ready to settle down.

Beverly and Hoover were working on a film entitled *From Russia with Love,* about windsurfing between islands in the Bering Strait, which bridges the closest points between the former Soviet Union and the United States. The landscape was apocalyptic, with bleak weather, strewn junk and houses with leaking roofs. Beverly, Mike, Arnold, a french Windsurfer, and the local Eskimos were the only ones for miles around.

Bev and Mike decided to get married on the beach facing the Soviet Union and told Arnold their intentions. Their ceremony was not to be a traditional one.

Hoover recounts Arnold's reaction:

> We told Arnold about our plans, and he responded, "Oh, that's impossible."

"Why?" we asked. "We already thought of it, you're a captain, and you can marry us."

"I'm not a captain."

"You have a windsurfer? Is that a boat?"

"Ah, but of course!"

So he put one foot up on the windsurfer and then he said some things that were very nice, very creative, very romantic and whatnot. Bev said some things too that were pretty thought provoking.

"It's like your foot," she said, "you may not like it as ya get older, but you're kinda attached." Warm, simple and we're both so serious we're shaking a little.

It was just the three of us and that was it. It was very low key. That's when *we* thought we got married.

Beverly wanted her own home with a garden, four kids, and time to watch them grow.

The couple maintained two houses, one in Los Angeles and one, (to which Bev had once been kidnapped), in Wyoming, just outside the Grand Teton National Park. In Kelly, Wyoming she had a garden, wanted a whole apple orchard, and the children who had not come yet. A postcard to her parents in the spring of 1980 revealed the split between her dreams and her reality.

5/3/80

We're getting ready for New Guinea—Current schedule: China until 27 May. Greenland, 8 June to 30 July—New Guinea August—September, October Antarctica. November 27 through January of 1981. Then it will be apple trees and babies.

For the next few years the apple trees and babies were on hold as Beverly and Hoover worked constantly on a variety of projects. She became more proficient at film making and in 1980 independently filmed an expedition of several Concordia college students as they skied across Greenland for the show, *American Sportsman*.

Photo from Mike Hoover's collection

Hoover had originally signed on to help film but took one look at the monotonous landscape they would be traveling across and decided not to go. Bev stayed with the project and, single-handedly filmed the entire trip. She had only her twelve foot pulk or sled to use as a dolly and had to change all her film in a portable black bag.

Shelly Addison, a young woman in 1980 and member of the Concordia expedition owed Bev more than a thank you for good footage by the end of the trip:

> I remember being rescued by my hair. I was being swept up in an Arctic Maytag cycle down an icy river, after falling in, and was unable to grab anything, the banks were sheer ice, two feet high.
>
> Beverly reached in and yanked me out of the cold waters by one of my braids, and while my adrenalin was pumping at Mach 1, Bev, as if describing peanut butter on toast said, "Sorry, honey if it's not on film it never happened."

The postmarks on Bev's letters throughout the early 1980s came from Greenland, New Guinea, Australia, Antarctica, Israel, the Soviet Union . . . Her tone in each contains the same peanut butter nonchalance, there is never a sense of self-importance or recognition of her exotic lifestyle. She had spent the last fifteen years deep in the climbing culture which assumed that people would seek out the exotic and challenging, so accomplishing it herself may have seemed to be nothing extraordinary. In 1981 a chronology of Bev and Hoover's travels lists over twenty-four different locations, sometimes they would work in three different countries within one week.

Reading the postcards that Bev sent home during 1980 is like looking into the windows of a passing train. Individually, they offer a snapshot of her experiences in each location. Viewed sequentially however, they chronicle the speed, precision, and effort of her life style required.

5/17/80

Hi, folks, I am back alive -

Mike is in Jakarta or Bali—I ended up with some business in Japan and came straight home afterwards—China was fascinating. Peking is bleak, the population seem underemployed and no hustle, but ready to go if there was any reason to.

Japan was a real pleasure—Business is formal, punctual and to the point—Everything works, everything's clean, people are polite—nothing's too much trouble. Lots of police about—the Bobby tradition sort—well respected, ready to help out—great subway system in Tokyo.

Sending you genuine Chinese prints, which there are doubtless millions around, but I thought they were pretty and you might enjoy them.

6/11/80

Flew to Greenland and back to Iceland—Plane couldn't land, same drill tomorrow—Reykjavik is what you would imagine— People are pleasant enough—lots of babies. Drizzling weather, eternal daylight.

Expedition members very amiable, not too hard core—99 tons of gear—Hi to all, Love you B

7/30/80

Hi folks and Randy -
Back alive [from Greenland]—That's a long walk—Mike opted out, being no dummy—I made the film which I think might be okay—heading directly for Wyo. from here, but should be in New York/Wash—mid August to edit so see you then . . . Can't get used to the heat, minus 20 on the ice cap—and windy. We had sails for the pulks (sleds) so they moved right along see you soon — Love B

8/25/80

. . . Friday leave for New Guinea (Irian Jaya it's called.) Looking forward to making my last parachute jump, otherwise it's completely uninspiring—Well, at least Mike wants to go—I think it's dumb to crawl around in a jungle, oh well . . . .

9/5/80

Jakarta-
Sorry we didn't get to talk longer, what a rush just to cool our heels here for a week with nothing to do but deal with the Indonesians (humorless Mexicans), to get papers in order for Irian Jaya. Cost of that to date, $7,000. Tomorrow we leave for Bali, a 12 hour trip in funky aircraft, then on to Irian on Sunday—at last. I'm Looking forward to being in the mountains, out of the heat, murk, and transvestites. Great team—should be fun—Should be done mid-October, then on to Australia and camels.
Love you—Look forward to coming home—Beverly.

* * *

Steamrolling through a stream of locations, landscapes, cultures and climates over the years took its physical toll. Beverly sustained several serious and countless minor injuries until she was tattooed with scars from bear bites, granite, barbed wire, and surgical stitches. She became practiced at surviving adventures, both of her own concoction and of Hoover's, though she wore the memory of each on her skin.

On location in 1980 for a film Hoover had put together, she almost became an amputee. Hoover had originally conceived of the show as an excuse to go to Australia to ride motorcycles. The concept was to document a camel round-up. Camels had been brought to Australia by the British as pack animals because they could tolerate the heat and subsist on anything. These camels were meticulously bred and their sperm was very valuable. The team was supposed to round up the camels, collect the sperm and try to sell it, documenting the entire process. ABC agreed to produce the project.

The trip produced a string of injuries. Hoover broke both his thumbs, another member broke his wrist, and Don Getz, one of the best motorcycle riders, dislocated his shoulder the first day.

After Getz hurt his shoulder, Bev agreed to ride his bike back for him. Although she could ride a bike, she had very little experience and didn't know to be wary of any posts, regardless of whether there was barbed wire visible or not. Often a the wire between posts has simply fallen down from disrepair, it's not gone. Hoover and Getz, preoccupied with Getz's injuries forgot to remind Bev of the dangers. Unfortunately she ran straight into some old barbed wire, her bike skidded out from under her, and the barbed wire spikes—acting like the teeth of a chainsaw—cut her foot almost completely off at the ankle. She spent the remainder of the trip in the Alice Springs hospital where a doctor spent an entire night cleaning the dirt and grime out of her foot. She required a series of operations to bring her foot back to working order, and although she would be able to walk and ski and climb moderate routes, the injury essentially ended her intensive climbing career. From that day on, she was never again able to put pressure on her ankle when it was in a twisted position, eliminating her ability to effectively use that foot in hard crack climbs.

Bev had always been accident prone, getting bruised and banged up when others didn't. Perhaps she simply had abused herself enough and got used to pain—growing up not being allowed to cry, no matter what—she rarely revealed the pain, going through recovery from even the most serious injuries without complains.

Malinda Chouinard, Beverly's friend from Yosemite Valley had stayed in touch with Beverly over the years and felt that often Bev's injuries were misinterpreted by the men Bev was with:

> What the men need to know is that they were wrong about Beverly. They think she was a masochist. She was always one of the girls, but to make her career she had to be better than all the guys.
>
> If Bev had been a man she would have been called "intrepid." As a woman her legendary injuries were badges of pride; proof of accomplishment. Bev couldn't wait to tell a story on herself, because her infirmities not only proved that her wild adventures were true, but also that she was a real lady, a delicate debutante who like, Nancy Drew and Wonder Woman, had escaped and prevailed yet again.

Hoover was also made aware that there was another layer to Bev's stoic nature. Speaking in 1995, he remembers that when he first introduced Bev to his mother, she told him, "Beverly is really, really exceptional, and if you're not careful you will break her, because she's just a little girl."

"BZZZZ, BZZZZZ..."

Bev and Mike held their formal wedding in Kelly on June 10, 1981. While the wedding was intended as a celebration, it required stamina and tolerance, as well as an open mind on Beverly's part. Hoover and Bev felt that they were truly married at the ceremony at the Bering Straight. This wedding, which took place in Grand Teton National Park was for their family and friends. In Hoover's mind it was really a formality, but for Bev, as the bride the day held a bit more weight.

Talking in 1995 and smirking like a kid for whom outsmarting the law is as easy and practiced as reciting Dr Seuss, Hoover tells the story:

> It was a whole epic in itself because I was late and almost got arrested. Me more than Beverly didn't take it that seriously. I was too callous, I should have been better, but I wasn't.

Before the ceremony Mike and a few of his friends decided to go and try out a new handgun that one of them had bought. They rode cross-country on their motorcycles out into the Park, to a place Hoover knew where they could set up a target and shoot. By now they'd already broken several Park rules, not the least being driving their motorcycles in the park.

Sure enough they soon noticed a Park Ranger's car coming towards them. They watched the Ranger, as Hoover puts it, "dressed in his full smokey-the-bear outfit and his little walkie talkie," pull over and look at them through his binoculars, and then begin to talk excitedly into his walkie-talkie.

Hoover and company leisurely packed up their gear, in no particular hurry, confident that on their motorcycles they could easily outrun the Ranger. They slowly started their bikes and headed off ready to lead the

Ranger on a wild goose chase. Hoover took off in the lead but as he rounded a corner,

> . . . I see a guy on a motorcycle coming right for us wearing a suit. It's a big guy, like he's a Park superintendent on a motorcycle.
>
> I'm thinking, "Damn these guys are good, how'd he get here so quick?!"
>
> I head for him for a while just to get a good look at him, and realized that the rider was my own brother Gary, who's up for the wedding, and he's wearing a suit, obviously. He'd come out to get me, so I wouldn't be late for the ceremonies.
>
> Now, so many times throughout his life this exact same thing would happen. He'd show up, and then he'd end up getting in trouble. As I go back he says, "Hey, hi, how 'ya doing?"
>
> I say, "The cops are behind us, turn around right away or you'll be arrested."
>
> "Not again, Mike, Not again!"

Gary did his best to keep up with Mike and his friends, until finally they made back to the cabin where Hoover was to get ready for the ceremony.

Bev, oblivious to the situation, was getting ready herself, and everyone else was starting to gather at the chapel.

As Hoover and the others got closer to the cabin they could see the Ranger cars closing in from the other direction. They ditched their bikes under a tree and made a run for it, getting into the cabin just in time.

As Hoover was dressing up for the wedding they could all hear the Rangers outside arguing about whether they should enter the cabin without a warrant. Caught inside Hoover could hear the Rangers as they communicated with each other on their radios. His heart sunk when he heard one voice; "We've got their motorcycles."

Eventually the Rangers left, and the groom, his brother, and friends, now all decked out for the wedding, rushed to the church. Hoover arrived a few minutes late to his own wedding.

Unfortunately the chase continued down the isle:

I'm walking down the aisle in this chapel and it's pretty well filled up—Mike Hoover recalls the events of his own wedding—and every place you look there were old friends I hadn't seen. About halfway down the isle there was a group of rangers who were friends of Bev's. She use to be a park ranger. They all got their radios on low and they're listening to something, bending over I can hear it, "Oh yeah, we have the motorcycles, but we are not sure if they went up or down river."

At the reception Don Getz, who owned two of the motorcycles, (and had worked with Bev and Hoover on the camel film in Australia) suggested that they try and talk with some of Bev's friends in the Park service to see if they can get the bikes back. Greg Patterson, head of law enforcement at the Park was at the wedding, so after hearing the story, Bev went off to try and find him, but it turned out he had already left. As the reception began breaking up Bev suggested they all go to Patterson's house and wait for him there. So the four of them Bev, Hoover, Getz and Braden, a friend of Hoover's who had been on the motorcycle chase, all went over to Patterson's cabin. Hoover knew that Patterson liked Bev a great deal. He figured it would be no big deal to get him to do a favor for her.

Beverly and Mike. Photo from family album, courtesy of Mr and Mrs Johnson.

So Bev, Hoover, and Braden all went to Patterson's place, they got inside, made themselves comfortable, and sat back to wait, while Getz, who had been thoroughly enjoying the reception punch wandered off.

Soon there was a knock at the door. Bev, Hoover and Braden were puzzled; "We did not hear a car drive up—Hoover explained—but maybe it was Patterson."

Bev got up and opened the door, and there was this ranger standing right in front of her. "Oh My God, . . . It's Getz!"

Getz had gone into the bedroom, and dressed up on one of Patterson's uniforms, his pants, his shirt, his hat. Now at the front door, facing the surprised Ms. Hoover he slurs out the words, "What seems to be the problem here?"

"Oh, Don, man, if Patterson comes home now and you're wearing his clothes, we'll never get those motorcycles back!"

"I don't know what you are talking about ma'm," Getz continues, "If you have been violating National Park laws, we will have your ass in a sling."

Bev comes to me and says, "Would you take care of him. OK?"

I don't know how I'm going to do that, Mike realls.

Bev says, "You guys just CUT THIS STUFF OUT, particularly you, Don. Don, just cut this shit out."

We took him in the bedroom and he put the stuff back on the hangers. We sat down and were waiting, and waiting, with no idea what time would Patterson get home.

All of a sudden we heard a small gasoline motor crank up. The unmistakable high pitch sound of a chain saw. Getz, no in possession of Patterson's chainsaw came into the house yelling over the motor noise, "Bev, what did you want cut out? How about this table?"

He went right down to the table with the blades whizzing, "Maybe I should cut this out over here, *bzzzzz, bzzzz bzzzz*, maybe we need a bigger door." He didn't touch anything, but he got very close.

"Get the chainsaw from him," Bev yells at me.

"Yeah, right."

I said to Braden, "Let's get the chainsaw."

Braden—"*You* get the chainsaw."

Getz is still buzzing next to everything and now there's smoke all over the room.

Then we hear a car drive up, and this time was Greg Patterson.

"Don," Bev said, "if you want to get your motorcycles back you will just get rid of the fucking chainsaw!" So he turned off the chainsaw, and Braden put it out back by the woodpile.

"Bev, go out and stall him," I said, "while I try to get all this smoke out of here."

Beverly turned to Don and said, "Don't do anything. You just lay low, don't say *anything*, just lay low."

She went outside, and you could hear her saying to Patterson, "Oh, what a nice car you have here! Is this a new radio?"

"Well, it's just a car," he answered.

"Well what is this, have they changed the nightsticks you guys use, do you use mace, is it a new kind of mace?"

He's looked at her as if thinking, "WHAT the fuck!?"

We were in there with the windows open, and finally it seems like it might be OK with the smoke. I went out to try to help stall him a while longer.

I had never met Greg Patterson before, so I said "Oh, I've heard so much about you!" We shake hands and, "Oh, nice car, is this a new radio?"

Then Braden came out and does the same routine, but now we were done stalling. "We have a problem, there was a little misunderstanding, maybe you can help us out."

We went back into the house but now there was no sign of Getz . . . there was this Navajo rug in the room, and there was Getz, spread eagled, under the rug, "Isth, thith low enough forth you Bev?"

Patterson looked at us like, "What the fuck is that?"

"Oh, that's just our friend, he had a little bit too much punch at the wedding," we explained.

We got the motorcycles back, and had to pay a $20 fine.

"I WANT TO DO THIS, I WANT TO FLY"

Bev was once heard to say that the greatest problems she faced came from the unexpected. Yet surly the unexpected and the unknown were also the most enticing for her. Her climbing and love for Antarctica, her relationships, her marriage all flirted the boundaries of dynamic, disastrous and sublime. The unknown was like garlic in her life, it increased the flavor, and soon enough, it was a staple ingredient. Deciding she wanted to learn to fly, therefore was somewhat of a natural progression.

Bev's initiation into the world of flight came during one filming session in Wimaea on the island of Oahu in Hawaii. Ed Cesar an accomplished pilot and hang glider had been working with Hoover for several years on a short film titled *UP* which captured the flight of a hang glider and the experience of its pilot. Bev and Ed had first met on the *Steadman* filming where Ed had worked as a crew member.

Ed, Bev and Hoover were in Hawaii along with Hoover's son Erik to do some filming with Erik. After they finished shooting, Bev asked if she could try out the hang glider, going double with Ed. She had studied hang gliding, and was very interested in the mechanics of ultralight crafts. Ed agreed to take Bev on a flight. They put on their helmets and strapped in. They would be flying tandem, side by side. Ed was on his guard because any sudden movements from Bev could jeopardize the safety of the flight.

"She just had a glow about her," Ed remembers. I was watching her and she was totally at ease. You could feel it in her body; she was totally relaxed.

We were up for maybe about an hour, not even that, floating around. Her first comment was how beautiful it was. I told her to look down between her feet because when you look down, there's *nothing* there, you feel like a bird. She just kept saying how pretty it was, and how good it felt. At that point something happens to you inside.

You could see her just let loose of a lot of stuff. When you're flying everything is completely simple, and she said, "I want to do this. I want to fly."

We landed on the beach, and she had a smile on her face that she couldn't get rid of. She couldn't stop smiling. She gave me a big hug, "Oh thank you, thank you."

It was like it came from every fiber in her body. It takes a while to come down from that. You're still thinking about being up there, flying, after you land. It's hours and hours before you lose the feeling.

Bev was hooked. Although she loved to hang glide she recognized the pragmatism in getting her pilot's license instead. Unfortunately, with all the various projects she and Hoover were working on she did not have the solid stretch of time she needed to learn properly. This changed when she bought a single engine Mooney airplane. With her own plane she could practice more intensely but she still ran into problems, and out of frustration she decided to call on Ed to help her. Ed began to teach her how to land the aircraft by explaining to her that first,

. . . you have never done in your life something that would enable you to judge a point up and down. It's not natural.

We went out part time for a week, I'd tell her, "OK, fly me six feet off the ground. Give me me three feet, ok give me six inches, touch the wheels to the ground.

The first time she did it, the plane was all over the place, so we went up and did low level stuff everywhere, over the water, over the mountains until she was real comfortable being close to surfaces and in control.

After this Ed taught Beverly how to fly by her wits and instinct as well as by the book, by showing her maneuvers not normally covered by the beginning flying courses. He worked her through the spectrum of potential disasters:

What happens if you pull the airplane up and you're looking straight down at the ground and the wind is down, what do you do? What is the airplane going to do? You're not taught that because of liability. But you're eventually going to run into it.

She learned that from 3000 feet you could glide thirteen miles back to San Pedro. We did it once, and decided that we'd leave the engine running next time because it was just too much pucker factor.

That sort of training is something they don't teach you in regular flying except briefly. You have to have your sense about you, and to know when to break the rules. And that's why you have mechanical-type pilots who fly by the numbers, and fly like a mechanic taking apart a car, step one, step two, step three. They don't teach real seat of the pants flying.

She felt a lot better after the week, and she went back and passed her test.

Beverly's plane, and piloting skills became a great resource to the filming-production company she owned with Hoover. She used the plane to scout for locations sites. They traveled frequently between Wyoming and Los Angeles in her single engine Mooney. She was good friends with the crews at the Jackson Wyoming airport, especially after she began bringing them her homemade brownies. When she had a free day she would pack up her dog Murphy, an Australian Shepherd/ Red Heeler mix, and fly to Yosemite in order to do a little climbing.

Alone in the cockpit Bev could enjoy a similar solitude as she had soloing El Cap. The plane engine transported her into the clouds. In the sky, alone, she was able to relax, and focus on the unexpected. The concentration required to fly, or climb offset the frenetic pace of production negotiations. Bev could soar solo unhindered, and maybe even get a chance to sit back and gloat at what it felt like to fly, and not fall.

Beverly experimented with different modes of flight. Trained as a smoke jumper to jump out of airplanes, and as an airplane and hanglider pilot, she is seeing here trying her hand on a motorized parapede. She briefly considered this type of equipment as an alternative to gyrocopter or ultralight plane as a scouting plataform.

Trying out the motor and harness for size. I can only wonder what their neighbors had to say about this scene.

"...ROUGH SEAS
AND PERIODIC BREAKDOWNS.
—AH, TOURING THE CONTINENT..."

Bev was hard-pressed to find serenity of any sort, especially not apple trees and babies, as 1981 brought a torrent of expeditions and work. The globe hopping had picked up the pace in late 1980 when Hoover and Bev were working on a film on sharks in the Red Sea for National Geographic. They were trying to get some footage of a fish called the Moses sole (which lives in the Gulf of Aqaba, an arm of the Red Sea between the Sinai Peninsula and Saudi Arabia), which is notable for its ability to repel sharks. They hoped to get the Moses sole in the act of repelling the shark on film. Each day they would set up all the equipment for the shoot, and position the Moses sole and the shark. Then they would release the shark into the sole's territory. Day after day, to their dismay and frustration, all that they could catch on film was the shark making lunch out of the sole . . . .

One day in the midst of this frustrating seagoing circus a rowboat came out to meet them. On the boat was an assistant to Armand Hammer with a telegram from the millionaire businessman and unofficial international diplomat. It stated simply;

"We need you to go to Antarctica immediately."

Although neither Bev nor Hoover had ever met Armand Hammer and barely knew who he was, they were aware of the expedition he was sponsoring. It was led by Ranulph Fiennes (now Sir Ranulph Fiennes), and was an attempt to circumnavigate the world from pole to pole. The Transglobe expedition, as it was called, had its own airforce, ship, boats, fleet of cars, and offices. Prince Charles, the patron of the expedition, had originally contacted Armand Hammer to ask him to contribute the fuel for the expedition. Prince Charles had also commissioned a film crew to document the trip. However, the expedition members and the film crew did not get along and Prince Charles turned to Hammer to find another film crew that could work in the challenging conditions the expedition would face. Hammer did not have to look far before he heard about Hoover and Bev.

The Transglobe expedition was, as Hoover said, "a monumental logistical undertaking, and in that respect it was fantastic. The doggedness was phenomenal, but in terms of physical exploration or adventure, there wasn't anything that hadn't been done many times before." Hoover told Hammer's assistant that they weren't interested.

Hammer though, was not easily dismissed. The next day the rowboat again appeared at the Red Sea production site. This time the telegram read:

"Imperative to have you immediately. **Name your price.***"*

Hoover was incensed that Hammer though he could be bought off but Bev saw the telegram in a different light. She reminded Hoover that they had certain things they needed money for, such as the house they hoped to build on their Wyoming property. She suggested that Hoover name some ridiculously high price, which if Hammer agreed to pay would make the work worth their time and effort. Hoover asked for double the highest amount he had ever been paid and gave his reply to Hammer's assistant.

The following day the rowboat returned with the reply,

"You've got it, come immediately."

At this point Bev and Hoover realized they would have to consider seriously the situation they were in. Although the money was tempting they had a contract to finish the *National Geographic* project. Then they had to envision getting off the boat they were on in the Middle East, flying back to Los Angeles, repacking all their equipment and traveling to Antarctica to meet the Transglobe expedition. They told Hammer's messenger to give his boss their sincerest regards but they would have to decline his generous offer.

The rowboat left, but the next day it came again, and this time Hammer had doubled his previous offer.

Bev and Hoover could not disregard this opportunity any longer. Soon the Moses sole and its ineffective shark repellent were half a planet away and the warmth of the Red Sea was only a memory.

Bev and Hoover had barely two days in Los Angeles before they took a plane to New Zealand. From there they traveled by boat to meet the Transglobe expedition in Antarctica. Bev was exhausted and worn thin by the constant travel. She came down with a flu when they were on the boat but bounced back by the time they reached the expedition.

Although Bev and Hoover got along well with the team, especially the leader, Ranulf Fiennes, they continue to feel trepidation about the expedition itself.

Bev wrote in one letter home, "They equate adventure with poor planning ." However, rather than being in the belly of a familiar beast, exploring and surviving as a small compact unit of a few self-sufficient people, on this trip they had a removed and more expansive perspective on the epic logistical battle of the Transglobe entourage. They were being paid handsomely for their time and for the most part, their survival was not in question.

One bright point for Beverly was her introduction to Giles Kershaw, who was working as a pilot for the Transglobe expedition. Giles had a reputation of being one of the best pilots in the world. He could fly anything from a 747 jetliners, to a gyrocopter, and was a pioneer in Arctic aviation travel. Giles and Bev connected with their love for the Antarctic, but even more they simply resonated with each other, and they were described as "two peas in a pod."

Bev sometimes mocked and occasionally marveled at the siege tactics the slow moving expedition used. She was burdened by the drudgery of the pace which was relieved only by moments of adventure and beauty. Bev recorded her experience on the Transglobe project in her letters home as she and Mike joined the expedition at various sites along its route. Her first letter, written in January, is from New Zealand, from which they were to leave for McMurdo Sound in Antarctica:

1/17/81

Hi folks,

. . . Trip down is moderately unpleasant; rough seas and periodic breakdowns plus the boat only does 8-9 knots in the best of circumstances. We have been lucky with the pack ice and should arrive in McMurdo in 3 or 4 days - then 20 days of skidooing around the ice cap then back in the boat and back home—Ah, touring the continent. The NSF is its usual hospitable self, but at least the New Zealanders are friendly. Prince Charles is the patron of the expedition so maybe it's just for the good of the Commonwealth . . .

Mike Hoover photo.

1/20/81

Docked in McMurdo this am. bright, sunny, cold. What a garbage dump—Ah, America—We have so much, we can make such a big garbage heap. Pretty dismal place compared to the peninsula. Think we staked our claim on the wrong side—waiting for the tractor to take us over to the NZ side—word is they have saunas, and a ski lift, ah wilderness . . .

In April, they were preparing for Canada:

4/25/81

I am working on Transglobe nearly full time which is no fun, and will be glad to see the end of it.—We've had to build special equipment for -50°F that has to be tested and refined. Plus food (you know what a joy that is) boats, tents (Antarctica revisited).

The problem is that we aren't going to Antarctica—instead it's a place just as cold, just as miserable (or possibly more so) with none of the compensations (except monetary.) Oh well . . .

In July she wrote from the Northwest Territory of Canada:

7/17/81

Hi folks -

A most uneventful trip—most excitement revolves around keeping various overloaded rental cars on the move—3 flats in 100 miles, rocks through the radiator—current vehicle works only in 4-wheel drive.

In a holding pattern here waiting for a Boston Whaler to be delivered to Inuvik. (Transglobe has given up on rubber boats) This may take a while . . . .

Mike is drawing up house plans for Kelly, hoping to do a lot with solar and hoping it will work.

Looks as though we won't be back 'til November, as all is delays and ifs. It's a good ice year and T.G. shouldn't have any trouble making it to Alert, though if they wait too long for this whaler, they may find it closing in on them—We have the impossible task of trying to keep up in our over-laden Zodiac which we intend to trade in on something faster, like a Jet Ranger (thank you Dr. Hammer).

It's nice in the North. We haven't been molested by bugs and the weather is mostly warm and sunny. Drove up the pipeline road to the Yukon River—excellent road lined with spindly black spruce—gentle, rolling hills—a big empty feeling. Flying over it, though there are surprising numbers of small settlements and meandering roads—So many bogs and lakes. Ah, the bugs. Glad not to be walking there . . .

Postal strike in Canada, so don't know when this will get to you . . . Love to all

In August they were at Resolute on Cornwallis Island in the Arctic:

8/22/81

74 degrees 43 deg. N - 94 deg. 57' W
Hi folks -
Nice hotel in Resolute, with every imaginable creature comfort, provided you stay inside. Expedition is beached in a south-facing bay by a South wind that has pushed the ice against the shore, so we're here 'til the wind changes or the fog lifts, or Thanksgiving, whichever comes first.

Expedition plods forward, slowly and uneventfully—so there's nothing to report—they don't leave the shore without our support, but this conservative approach has been at the expense of squandering some good conditions and the short season and now the ice is beginning to reform, so they must hurry on or spend yet another year—a fate that they accept casually.

Otherwise the Arctic is thoroughly enjoyable—and I am sorry to be in this comfortable hotel as there is so much to see.

We camped on Somerset Island last week—strange beauty to these islands. Far north of the tree line, past the shrub and bush line—with just occasional tundra, the islands are mostly just limestone rubble, seemingly arranged by a demented D-9 cat driver—How the animals eke out a living is amazing—It's a desert.

We tracked a polar bear away from Camp—Footprints in the fresh snow—just to make sure that he wasn't up to some treachery, like circling around and popping in on camp unannounced, something P-bears are reported to do. But it appeared he had drifted in with the ice and having no interest in us had walked to the end of the Bay and caught an iceberg out. We have seen many seals, so he probably wasn't too hungry. I don't worry too much about bears, though it's necessary to keep your eyes open and your gun handy—which you want to do anyway just for the sake of a Caribou dinner.

Went for a boating trip with some Eskimos (or Inuit as they call themselves). We had intended to film but the locals pulled in at the first sign of rough water.

The highlight of the trip was the erection of the tent, a dome shaped affair that was inflated with a bicycle pump and appropriately called an igloomatic. The tent was for sale, and the owner was attempting to demonstrate the ease of putting it up, but was thwarted by a stiff breeze which would continually flatten the tent despite ardent pumping. After much laughter and the loss of a sale, everyone pitched in and guyed it out. The end result was quite good and we sat inside and had tea and caribou stew and waited for the weather to improve which it didn't, so we returned to the bad weather and darkness.

Mike joined Transglobe's Boston Whaler to continue the journey with them. As there wasn't room for me (for which I was secretly grateful, though feeling quite guilty) I went on to Resolute, a community which owes its location to a freighter that, unable to reach Melville Is. with the basic materials for building the settlement, dumped them on the beach here—and here it is. The airstrip is fog bound most of the summer and it's not unusual for the pilots to land on the beach and walk to town when the airport is closed. Fog lifts and there's otters parked all over.

Feeling like it must have been in the good 'ole days of aviation, before the FAA and computers started flying—Evenings, eaves-dropping on pilot talk, think of Dad, how well he'd fit—what a good time they're having with their planes. Twin Otters. 100 steps with no big ditches is a landing strip—then there's fog and wind and ice, so there are many good times, many stories . . . .

8/24/81

Snowing out—days getting noticeably shorter—sun now sets and it's nearly dark in the middle of the night. Sun sets for the winter in late October in northern Ellesmere so the lads had better get cracking or they'll be stumbling around in the dark.

There's a plan afoot to leave tomorrow morning—the ice is out, fog is in. But whatever the problems, they manage to pull it off, or rather buy it off, and that gets a lot of credit—nothing stops them.

Mike and I are going to fly north rather than sally forth in the Zodiac, which would be both pointless and impractical. We'll walk and ski up Ellesmere with them, which ought to be an enjoyable outing.

Then back to Wyoming. Would like to get this house built or at least roofed and framed before winter . . . .

It was in October, when the crew was at Point Alert on Ellesmere Island in the Northwest Territories of Canada—1200 miles north of the northernmost point in Alaska—that Bev began to feel bad. Despite increasing pain she kept going until her body simply surrendered. She had a ruptured ectopic pregnancy, an often fatal condition. In an ectopic pregnancy, the fetus attaches itself to the fallopian tube instead of dropping into the uterus. As the fetus grows it puts pressure on the fallopian tubes and internal organs, causing extreme pain. At the point when the tube ruptures there is severe internal bleeding. At the time Beverly suffered the rupture it was late at night and a snowstorm had started. She managed to make it on foot to an Army hut where she collapsed on the bed and lay twisted in pain moaning at the slightest movement. Hoover retrieved the local doctor who worked for the Canadian military. The doctor took one look at Bev and said, "Ma'm, I am not the Lord."

With Bev writhing in agony Hoover went to Giles in the hopes that he could get her to help. Giles checked the flight schedule in Resolute, which was still terribly far away, but saw that if they hurried they could make one of the few commercial flights that flew out of Resolute.

He put all the fuel he had into the plane and with Bev and Hoover inside, he took off. The flight was an epic, navigation through the storm was sheer guesswork and the ice building on the wings could have downed them at any time. Giles radioed ahead to make sure the plane would be held if they were late. With Beverly fading in and out, going from horrible to not so bad Giles landed and they made the connection.

Despite her condition Bev refused to see any other doctor than the one she knew in Los Angeles. When the plane arrived there she was taken directly from LAX to Huntington Memorial Hospital where she was operated on immediately. She was full of blood internally, according to Hoover, and the doctors were amazed she was still alive.

Bev survived, but at thirty-four her body was becoming a testament to the the difference between the limitations of the body and the mind. While her spirit could keep going sometimes her body just couldn't. The ruptured ectopic pregnancy put her dream of apple trees and babies in jeopardy. The house in Kelly, Wyoming, a small town right outside Jackson Hole with a panoramic view of the Grand Teton Range, did get built in November, but with the ectopic pregnancy she had lost essentially one whole side of her reproductive system.

Beverly was close to Hoover's children, Erik and Holly, but she and Hoover had always assumed that they would have children at their own as well. Early in their relationship Bev had gotten pregnant accidentally. They decided that it was not a good time to start the new family, and they opted for an abortion. With some remorse Hoover explains:

> That was a mistake because in a way, it's never a good time. It's a very invasive little creature you're bringing into your home and it's going to take a lot of your time and it's going to change your life. So that's never going to change, and we made a mistake. We had it aborted and that was very hard on her.
>
> Later on she told me that she knew deep down it was the wrong thing to do. As it turned out it was wrong, because it was probably

a very healthy baby. The doctor had to do the abortion twice, it was a tenacious little guy.

They continued to try and have kids. Bev went through invitro fertilization therapy taking high doses of hormones which wracked her entire system. More intense was the emotional drain of having to repeatedly go through a cycle of hope and disappointment. She appeared to be unable to conceive. Furthermore, after one ectopic pregnancy her risks of having another if she became pregnant again were high, and this time she most likely would not survive. Though her body had brought her to many places and expanded her world in many dimensions, it could not provide her the experience of mothering a child of her own.

"Oh, That Is Soo Kind of You"

For some people parenting is instinctual, and Bev had the heart of a mother. If she could not have children of her own she found others to watch over, and with each film project there was inevitably someone in need of guidance, and occasionally a rescue. "What she didn't have, the children, she made up for in many other ways," a friend recalled. "She was always parenting and teaching."

Mike Graber had recognized this in Bev once when she came to rescue him and Rick Ridgeway in Yosemite. Her timely help continued to be a saving grace in the other expeditions they shared. As Hoover's partner Bev drew on her ability to guide people through difficult situations and to apply the right amount of support, encouragement or challenge at the right time. Malinda Chouinard noted that Beverly and Mike Hoover's relationship was;

> . . . an enduring truce and a great symbiotic partnership. Hoover is impossible, impatient, creative, and quick tempered. Bev was proud of being a brave 19th century explorer type wife; diplomatic, charming, forgiving and intrepid.

Bev was able to be the diplomat to Hoover's dictator, ameliorating situations he ignited with his temper and translating what he needed done to those he could not communicate with. In this way as a wife, Bev was very traditional. Where Hoover was most often the primary cameraman, she learned the intricacies of working the sound equipment and complementing him to create a filmmaking team. Her commitment to and love for Hoover was absolute. While he could become obsessed with various projects, for her, he came first above all else.

A close friend of theirs, Rick Jacobs, met Hoover and Bev when he worked for as Armand Hammer's personal assistant. Jacobs was struck by the way he saw the two of them work together:

> I think that as many accomplishments as she had in her life she would choose one and that was being married to Mike. Because she really loved the guy and it was clear in everything that she did. She was interested in keeping him balanced, in being with him, in enjoying life, but with him, in a very committed way.
>
> I remember watching the two of them work as an incredible team. Mike was, literally, out front with his camera, and then there was Beverly with the sound boom.
>
> Mike would just trust absolutely and completely in her. The way you could tell was that wherever they were he'd be filming away and he'd just start backing up, didn't look where he was going because he was looking into the camera, and she just guided him, they were just like one. She would kind of hold his rear end or whatever and you didn't notice it except it was incredible.
>
> In my mind that was how they were, as one. She knew exactly where he should go, what he should do. I can't imagine focusing through the lens of the camera and backing up and moving around, no jerking, no bumping, Bev would just be moving things ever so smoothly, probably really guiding him. Probably she was pushing him in certain directions.
>
> One night I called her in Wyoming and we were just talking and she said, "I'm up on the roof."
>
> I said "What?"
>
> "I'm giving Mike a weather station."
>
> So she was up there on the roof by herself at like 10 o'clock at night installing this whole weather station. For her that would have been like walking behind him holding him, making sure that the pictures came out right. That was everything for her in a lot of ways.
>
> In my mind her primary accomplishment in her life was the two of them.

Don't get me wrong, she stuck by her guns, but she would have done the most in terms of accommodating and ameliorating. She knew what she wanted and most of the time what she wanted was what Mike wanted.

As Hoover's perfectionism and temper preceded him so did Bev's diplomacy and her ability to quietly take care of everything so that each person could get their job done in the best way. What Hoover wanted done on a production, how the equipment was to be set up and labeled, his ways of organizing a shoot and producing a film, were the rules everyone followed. Beverly became fluent in translating Hoover's desires to those he worked with, becoming a conduit through which his precise instructions could be understood and made clear to those he worked with even when he himself wasn't able to communicate exactly what he wanted.

After working with them both over the years Mike Graber was witness to this dynamic in action several times.

Beverly had done so many films with Hoover she knew how Hoover liked to do things. I was often hired as a second camera guy. I would show up and Beverly would say, "We should label the magazines like this, we need this much information on the film cans."

I can remember a couple times going, "Nope I know how to do this," like, you do your job, I'll do mine, and that was how I kinda felt.

But really she knew, she'd been through the drill so many times with Hoover, that she knew how he wanted things done. She was just trying to save me getting yelled at by Hoover, for not doing it his way.

There were some negotiations where fundamentally Hoover's approach did not work, but Beverly's would. For instance, Mike Graber remembers negotiations to shoot an IMAX film on caving in South Africa:

They wanted to do an IMAX film exploring caves. IMAX films are usually funded by museums, and there's a group of theater owners that will pool their money to produce a film.

There's this museum in the Midwest somewhere that's dying for this caving film. They've got the contract and everything and they're just about to sign, the guy has the money, wants to give it to Hoover.

The museum curator, says, "You know what I think would be a real nice opening to this film? You start in a museum, with a museum curator, and the guy is showing you a map of this or that . . . ."

Hoover is listening to this, and Beverly's sitting here too, and here's their two approaches. Bev: You either listen to the guy, you go, "Oh yeah, that's a real good idea," and then once you get to filming you pitch that.

Then there's the Hoover approach.

He says to the guy, "The way films are made you have a film maker, who knows how to make films, and you have a producer who knows how to find the money. You're the producer, and I'm the film maker. Now when one of us thinks they are better at the other person's job, it fucks everything up. If you think you know how to make films, that screws up my job, I can't do my job. If I think I know where the money should come through, you can't do your job."

Emphasis with Hoover, right hand karate chop into the left, "That's [flap] the way [flap] it works."

They never got the money.

Beverly's said, "Mike, you completely fucked up, we could have had the money and everything."

But Hoover's approach is, "All I did is nip it in the bud, it was going to be a problem anyway and if that lecture was enough to make those guys back out, then it saved us headaches in the long run." So he may be right but that wouldn't be Beverly's approach.

Beverly could win over anyone. If it was a situation where you had 4,000 pounds of camera equipment that you needed to get into Argentina, and you had a customs officer that wanted to make sure that it didn't, Beverly could win him over.

Beverly's sincerity often was tempered by a dramatic flair that airports and customs officials brought out in her. Her empathy often won her the hearts of those she whose support or approval she sought, but when it came to customs and airports a certain theatrical panache surfaced and as Hoover said, "it was almost like a game." Their cops and robbers Wyoming wedding was evidence that Bev could play Bonnie to Hoover's Clyde, but Bev's solo improvisations in airports were her *tour de force*.

London's Heathrow airport at three in the morning on a midweek, midwinter night was the stage for one of Bev's most memorable performances. Bev, Hoover, Mike Graber, and Ron Peers (who had worked with Hoover and Bev on the Transglobe expedition) were returning from a project in Afghanistan and arrived, in an exhausted heap of dirty bodies and cases, boxes, and packs full of expedition and film equipment. They had to get cleared through customs so that the film they had made could be taken to the CBS office in London.

With their tolerance thinner than a communion wafer they could only pray that the officials would let them through without a hassle. Unfortunately, they were given "the full stop," recalls Hoover. The official informed them, "I'm sorry sir the customs office closes at this time and this stuff can only be received into bond. Once it's held in bond you can proceed to gate 17B, at which time you will be cleared for your passport. You can perhaps get a motel room, and then tomorrow at 10:30 you can come back . . ."

It was Bev's time to take the spotlight. She told Hoover, Graber, and Peers to wait by the baggage. They did and promptly fell asleep. Then, through a dreamy haze Hoover remembers hearing what he recognized as Bev's voice getting louder and louder. He open his eyes to see Beverly coming down the hall sitting in a wheelchair that was being pushed by a customs official.

Hoover quickly woke up the other two and told them to play along.

Beverly and her escort came up to them and the men were greeted by a look of disgust from the custom's official which made obvious that he thought they were lower than any paleolithic worm. It was clear he felt they should be ashamed that while they had waited in peaceful slumber their poor disabled female companion had been forced to take care of everything.

In the most meek of voices Beverly looked up at the official and said:

"Well, these gentlemen are just so helpful, but they are very tired, and I don't think we can count on them for too much help, I could probably do it"

Rising to the occasion the official replied, "I'll get some of my men and we'll move this equipment *immediately.*"

"Oh, that's soo kind of you." doted the "helpless" Bev.

While the official got on the phone to rally his troops Bev gave Hoover one look which said "Keep Quiet."

The men with carts came and began loading on the baggage. Hoover, Graber and Peers were treated as the dirtbags they were assumed to be.

With the train of baggage carts leading the procession Beverly, cooed over the gallant official:

"It's so wonderful of you to do this, I'm so lucky to have met you." The official pushed Bev along behind her entourage and left the three men alone in the hallway with only a scowl of distaste.

After they had been taken through customs with the red carpet treatment and signed off, Peers and Graber turned to Bev in redemption, and pleaded, "Ooh, please Bev, can I please push your wheelchair?"

Bev had the opportunity for another performance at the Los Angeles International Airport as they were leaving for a project in New Guinea. They had forty-three cases with them containing everything from food and camera and climbing equipment to ice climbing gear and hammocks to use in the jungle. When Bev, Hoover and the three or four others traveling with them arrived at LAX, the airport was jammed. Again, she took center stage. With her clipboard in hand she went to the desk and panted, as if she was out of breath, "I need to speak to the manager right away."

"Sorry ma'm," the man behind the desk said "we're very busy but if you stand in line . . ."

"You don't understand," she pleaded, "we have an emergency. Right now I need to speak to the manager."

The man went and got the manager who in turn asked Bev what he could do for her.

"You have to hold the plane," she demanded, "the plane cannot take off. The flight that goes to Australia, it can't leave. I have 17 people coming, the traffic is unbelievable, they're not going to get here in time, we have all this baggage here and stuff to try to get on the plane, by the time they get here . . . If you don't hold the plane, the tour won't happen, they'll demand a refund, and I'll lose my job!"

In a calming tone the manager replied that instead of holding the plane, possibly he could have the tourist's baggage checked through so that when the group arrived they could go straight to the gate and board.

"That's impossible, you have to hold the plane," Bev emplored, but then added, as if with the most reluctance, "but let's check everything in first too."

So while Bev filled out the baggage tags several porters came over to load up the cases. The weight limit was sixty-five pounds. Several of the cases weighed over one hundred pounds so as soon as Bev realized what was going to happen, she pushed in between the porter and the case, "That's OK I'll get it," and she made a move to carry the case away as if it were full of feathers, trying to act like it was no big deal.

After loading all the baggage on (without paying the overweight extra charges) Bev and the rest of the expedition got on the plane.

"Have you heard from them, are they coming?" the manager asked as they boarded

"Oh yeah, the other people . . . uh . . ." Bev stalled "They will be coming, and I'll have them look for you. Thanks a lot for helping, it's really good of you."

The amount of equipment Bev and Hoover required for each production was often the biggest obstacle they had traveling. Although they personally could survive on very little, any film production demanded the appropriate equipment as did any climbing expedition. This problem was acute when they traveled to Antarctica. On one trip their luggage included a gyrocopter, a very light helicopter which can be disassembled. When the expedition crew arrived for their flight to South America it was Bev who approached the desk. She introduced herself, and Hoover described how the scene played out:

She said, "We're the people who are with the expedition that has the complementary baggage from," (She had the name of the president of the airlines which she just found from looking at the airline magazine where it says *"we at XYZ Airlines always believe that courtesy was the most important. . .* signed president whoever."

It's ten at night, and the lady behind the desk looks at Bev kinda funny and yells behind her.

"Oh, hey Bob, you know anything about the complementary baggage going to South America?"

"No."

Beverly says, "Oh, I'm sure it's in the fax or something, it's on somebody's desk or something, you probably weren't here this morning. You guys weren't here this morning were you?" It's ten o'clock at night, *of course they weren't here this morning."*

"No."

"Well, that's when he apparently talked to the manager here or something, I don't know how that works."

So they go look around for a fax, and Bev says, "My, that's very strange, I have the president's home number, maybe you could call him . . .gee that'd be kinda late, but hey, Mike, see if you can find his home number, you know it was on that list of contacts from the airline."

I start to go through my bag, "Yeah, I got that number here somewhere."

Time is ticking away and this guy comes out and looks at all our stuff, "All this stuff's going on this flight, that's going to take up time."

"Well then, we'd better get it loaded," Bev says. "You guys can just call him, you must have his number at home for emergencies."

Though they left their names and numbers with the airline, they never got the bill for the extra baggage.

"IS THERE ANY GREAT DISTINCTION AMONG INFIDELS?"

In November of 1982, Hoover began documenting the Soviet occupation of Afghanistan. He and his film crew were sponsored by various news organizations, including ABC, who also aired their coverage on the *American Sportsman* show. The November trip was the first of many to Pakistan, Afghanistan and the Soviet Union. Over the next five years these assignments would demand total concentration, and would dominate Beverly and Mike's lives.

Hoover was compelled by the Afghan rebels' struggle and came to see the Afghan war as the Russian Vietnam. In the late 1980's, through their friendship with Armand Hammer, Bev and Hoover were able to negotiate with the Soviet military to document the war from the Soviet's perspective as well. Beverly spoke fluent German and could get by in several other languages. As she worked covering the Soviets she began to teach herself Russian as well. On several occasions she and Hoover would have camera crews filming from both sides during one battle.

For Hoover the war and its politics became a personal passion and an obsession. Bev grew to have a love-hate relationship with Afghanistan. For her the war itself seemed pointless, the dangers not worth the price in a country whose rigidly patriarchal religion she believed would be its Achilles heel. Yet, she could not resist the urge to help the people whose lives were being destroyed even as she was filming them.

When their involvement with Afghanistan was just beginning Beverly and Hoover met MJ Koreiva who, at the time, was working for a computer company. MJ was able to help them obtain one of the first laptop computers produced. Not long after that MJ began assisting them with the logistics of production and ultimately became a veritable basecamp manager for their production company in Los Angeles.

MJ, a tall athletic woman with a photographic memory and a tenacity for tracking down details, helped to juggle the thousands of intricacies every trip required, from collecting rolls of duct tape, to obtaining the necessary and correct Visas. MJ never traveled with them to Afghanistan, her expertise lay in negotiating the terrain in Los Angeles.

MJ was one of the few other women integral to Hoover and Bev's productions—she often stayed in Hoover and Bev's house when they were away and several times while they were in town—she developed a close friendship with Beverly, and had a window into Bev's life that Hoover and the other male associates did not.

* * *

The extensive outdoors and travel experience of Bev, Hoover, and their film crews was taxed to the limit on the Afghanistan productions. Constant bombing and gunfire accompanied them all the time. Poor or insufficient food and water stretched their physical tolerance. Dysentery was normal, hepatitis to be expected. Beyond the physical, their mental stability was strained as they repeatedly bore witness to the havoc war wreaks on its participants. After she and Hoover began documenting the war from the Soviet perspective, Bev wrote in her journal of her experiences traveling in a Soviet APC (armored personnel carrier):

> I had become conscious of my thoughts and was wondering why I was choosing these particular visions as my last ones.
>
> "Probably just a breakdown up ahead"—Mike, the good husband, allaying the anxious wife. It did not account for the automatic weapons fire.
>
> "Traffic is still moving north." No need to worry, when the *Mujahedeen* [the Afghani rebels] wasted a convoy, they crashed a bus at one end, crashed a bus at the other and pick off what was in between. In this case, us.
>
> But the setup wasn't right. That's an ambush for a narrow canyon, not an open plain. Baghram airbase is close by. Close

enough. The road is well defended. More automatic weapons were fired, some rockets, close but not that close. Things were not improving. The traffic was no longer heading north.

Mike looked impassive. The kid on the turret gun tensed, this was not a good sign. I was looking around in the dim light, trying to assess the seriousness of what was happening, trying to gauge it from their eyes. Kid's eyes, intent eyes, Russian eyes. I looked out the tiny slit that serves as a window in an armored personnel carrier

Looking for *Baghram*, hoping for jets. MIGS (Russian built jets) puking flares to ward off the Stingers (American made ground to air missiles). MIGS to chase off the ambushers.

Mike Hoover photo

But there was nothing but the blue Afghan sky above and by the road, charred truck carcasses, bombed buildings, deserted orchards. "The earth is hard and heaven far," a regional saying. That is what I was thinking about when I wondered why I am thinking about it. Why the sky in Afghanistan seems so far away.

I gave passing consideration to why we had not executed our plan. Mike and I had discussed the ambush possibilities in the leisure of the Kabul Hotel dining room. The plan was simple: when the shooting starts, jump off the APC and lie flat in a ditch. At least we would not become Spam-in-a-can. We forgot to make allowances for the different scenarios. The ditches were already full of hostile locals who would not understand, that in spite of the Russian uniforms we were really American journalists. Not that they would care.

Russian rockets went one way, American rockets came back. They are the victims, their land, themselves. Is there any great distinction among infidels?

Besides at the point when we could have jumped, before our Russian hosts starting stuffing us down the hatches, the trouble was just a distant *rat atat atat*. Time passes, a lot of time. The APC is stuffy but not hot.

It is late November, nearly Thanksgiving. The interior of the personnel carrier is painted a pleasing beige. So is the exterior. I study the hatch mechanism as a design problem. The solution was not particularly elegant but like everything else on the vehicle it looked rugged. Rockets, unfortunately, go through APCs like butter.

More *rat atat atat*. I think I should be thinking about home, but my mind can no longer leave Afghanistan.

Farhat's patient. The patient was a young mother. She came from Kunar province. She lived with her inlaws because her husband had been killed in *Jihad*, two of her brothers were fighting in the war, the other two already dead. She had three children. A boy, who was five, another child about three and a small baby. In the fall the village was bombed. From her family, only she and her children survived, because they were away when the MIGS came.

Together with the other survivors they started for the refugee camps in Pakistan. Many were wounded, all were weak. They took only what they could carry. In the end the journey would take a month.

They could not travel directly, but had to cross the mountains in Nuristan. The mountains rise to 20,000 feet and it was already snowing there. The group moved slowly, but the mother often had to carry the three year old as well as the infant. No one could help her, no one had strength.

. . . many were wounded. All were weak.
Mike Hoover photo

After one week, the five year old son became sick. In a few days he was too sick to walk, so the mother carried him as well.

In the mountains, she could no longer carry all three. She took the infant and wrapped him as snugly as she could and left him in the snow beside the trail, hoping that someone would find him before the wolves did, although there was little chance of it. She took the other two children and went on.

After three hours, she could go no farther. She begged the leader of the group to turn around, she couldn't leave her baby. The leader refused, but offered to camp so that she could return, even though it was pointless.

The mother went back to the spot where she had left her baby. It was blue and very cold. He didn't move or even seem to breathe. She tucked the tiny body into her dress and started back for the camp. She felt him move. He was alive. She carried the three children to Pakistan. It took 20 days. It is the only story I heard in the camps with a happy ending.

There is Russian chatter. Hatches pop open and the Major clambers out for a look around. The radios either aren't working or there is no one up front to respond. The Major heads off for the front of the column.

I figure I'll check it out too. Maybe execute the ditch plan if things go badly wrong. People are milling around. Most of the convoy is civilian, mainly supplies headed south, some military hardware headed north. I scrambled up on a nearby truck . . . .

Bev's ability to exude calm in situations that begged for panic made her an ideal crew member *in*-country. One friend compared Beverly's reporting on the tumultuous surroundings in Afghanistan to the classic imperturbable British explorer walking into a jungle and respectfully taking note of the incredible flora and fauna, except instead of flowers it was the broken bodies and burned villages. Torn between her humanitarian sympathies with the Afghanis and her sense of the pointlessness of the war, Bev was never as obsessed with documenting it as Hoover was. She helped to support him emotionally, and financially through the film and sound work she did back in the U.S., but the motivation for the work in Afghanistan came primarily from Hoover.

* * *

When Bev was back in the United States working on other projects she still was vital as a safety net for the crew members in Afghanistan. They often found themselves in situations which required assistance from someone on the outside.

One time Hoover had come down with a severe form of crippling arthritis related to the dysentery he had. He was stranded in a remote village unable to walk. Bev at that time was in the United States. After trying unsuccessfully to reach Hoover by phone, during their pre-arranged phone times, she packed her things and flew to Afghanistan. Upon arrival she followed the few leads she could get, asking if anyone knew where to find a 6'4" American journalist carrying large video cameras. She was able to track down Hoover, and arrived in the village he was staying in with a small camel caravan. To get back to proper medical treatment they would have to cross a desert which would expose them to severe Soviet bombing. They waited two anxious days for the bombing to decrease, then she packed the equipment, and Hoover, up on the back of a camel and led him back across the desert. They were bombed several times but not hit, and Hoover made it to the U.S. for medical treatment. After a lengthy convalescence he fully recovered, but Beverly was more convinced than ever that this was a war not worth dying for.

Rick Jacobs, who helped Hoover and Beverly in their negotiations with the Soviets in Afghanistan, recalls:

> Beverly consistently said that the bad news about Afghanistan was really not the Soviets, it was the Afghanis. She said that the Afghan men were so screwed up in the way they were doing things that they were going to ruin their own country, and in a certain sense the Soviets and the Communists there had a better way of looking at things, than this violent, religionistic view on the world that the Mujahedeen [the Afghani rebels] had.
>
> That was sort of amazing that she would say those things in 1987 '88, when people were not in love with the Soviets. If you look at history, she was right.

As a woman and a film maker there were more doors open to Bev in Afghanistan then to Hoover or any of the other male crew. Hoover relied on her to give the women's perspective on that otherwise closed aspect of Afghani society, and she developed a deep admiration and love for the Afghani women.

Bev understood the Afghani women, who had to live and function in a culture that did not believe they were equals. Bev though highly respected and admired, spent most of her time and energy in a professional field dominated by men. This afforded her another lens through which she could empathize with the Afghani women, and gain a closer perspective and understanding of their plight. For Bev the Afghani women's pragmatism and courage highlighted the men's fanaticism and machismo stupidity.

Hoover, speaking in 1995, reflected on Bev's Afghanistan experience and her perspective:

> She had a much better grasp on the society than I did. And she just loved the women, they were so wonderful, so powerful and strong and smart.

There was one scene when we were staying with some Afghan friends and the buses came for more young men to fight. Many of these young men, almost boys, had really spent much more time in the refugee camps in Pakistan than they had in Afghanistan. But they had heard all these stories about Afghanistan and they were excited about the fight, the battle, off to war, *Jihad*, holy war.

These very spectacular, gaudy, elaborate buses with jewelry hanging off of them, with real loud crazy horns, have arrived and the young men are going off to war. They're so excited, just jumping and running around. Bev and I were watching and filming.

In the background were the moms. The women were not supposed to be seen. But they're watching their babies going off to fight. They're drawn like magnets to their boys. They were openly crying. You could see their faces, as they came right out into the street sobbing, creeping closer and closer to the young men.

The mores of society were holding them back, and the love for their sons were pulling them forward. They wanted—seemingly— to tell their boys "Don't do it, don't go, war it stupid, this is dumb and ludicrous."

It's the classic age-old thing where the men are going off to start the "My dick is bigger than yours" sort of thing and the woman's perspective is, "Are you guys out of your mind?" Yes, they are.

It was such a graphic illustration of this and Bev and I are filming it all. It was the same exact thing that's happened for thousands of years, the same mechanism. The mother love, the strongest emotion in the world, for these idiots who cared about their mothers but wouldn't show, or respond to their pleads.

That's the long way of saying part of Bev's looking at the war in Afghanistan was, "It's so stupid," and it's so stupid for *me* to go over there.

It was a unique situation for us because it was an opportunity to tell the story. That this was the Russian Vietnam. We believed that those people, like the Vietnamese, could repel the Russians out of their land.

What really did it, wasn't the Afghanis muskets or the Vietnamese pungy sticks, it was the press. We would hold up our cameras and say, "This is the most powerful weapon on the face in the earth."

For Beverly, in a sense what I was doing over there was sort of the same. There's the same excitement, the same drama and macho, and it wasn't really that much different than the whole event. She'd think wouldn't it be more intelligent in the long run to avoid the whole arena, because to get killed over there for something that was as foreign as it was stupid.

So there was that side, and there was the side that once she was over there and knows the people, she wants to help.

As soon as you point a camera you skew the subject, it's like the Heisenberg uncertainty principle. You can't look at it without affecting it. You've got a bunch of Afghanis sitting around with guns and stuff, as soon as you take out your camera, they're posing and yelling and running around. You want to start a riot? Bring out the cameras. There was certainly some of that in what we saw.

So what worked for Bev was understanding it was their problem, not hers.

As soon as you point a camera . . .
Photo by Mike Hoover

Bev was in a unique position because as an American and a member of the film crew she could sleep, eat and travel with any of the American men. As a women she was allowed access into the shrouded universe of the Afghani women. She also found some sanctuary in being part of the hidden world of Afghani femininity. Malinda Chouinard loved to hear the stories Bev told her of her time with the Afghani women, and how she would wear the traditional concealing robes of the Afghani women, the

Chador. Malinda remembers Bev was not always adept at being a traditional woman:

> Bev liked to wear *Chador*. She delighted in the ability to hide from strange men and never had to worry about a bad hair day. Yet, this garb was hard to manipulate. One evening, when she was sitting demurely in *Chador*, the only woman at dinner, she arose to excuse herself but the tablecloth mixed with her veils and she pulled the whole dinner to the floor. By her account, those present graciously accepted this awkward Westerner and actually thought it quite hysterical.

Being a bridge between the two genders also put pressure on Bev as a cultural translator.

Often Bev would eat with the women in the villages they stayed in because it was assumed to be bad karma if she ate with Hoover and the other men. After dining with the women Bev would return to sleep with Hoover and the rest of the crew. Intrigued about the forbidden female half of Afghani society which they were expressly forbidden to explore, the American men would grill Bev about her experiences with the Afghani women. Once Bev returned from dinner and explained that each time they would do something for her they would say "piggy piggy." She figured the women had given her the nickname, "piggy" because they thought she ate a lot. It was only later that Bev learned that in Pashto, the principal every day language of Afghanistan, "puigut" means, "Do you understand?"

Navigating the cultural differences and translating the expectations and traditions that went beyond language barriers was rarely an innocuous task, especially in a war zone. When arriving in any foreign country Bev and Hoover would try to talk with the ex-patriots they could find. Often they could get better information from the people who had lived for years in that particular culture than from any academics they spoke with before or during the trip.

In Afghanistan one of the most frustrating problems they encountered was the Afghani's attitude about time. Hoover explains their situation:

The Koran says, you should always dress in a way that's respectful to your fellow man. So everybody dresses very modestly. Koran says you will dress in a *sharwal camisse*. To dress in any way that makes you stand out is being disrespectful to somebody that's not as fortunate as you. Good idea really.

When you go on *Haj*, when you go to Mecca, which every Muslim is required if possible and if he can afford it, to go to Mecca once in his lifetime, and the trip is called the *Haj*. When they go on *Haj*, it's specified in the Koran that you cannot wear anything that even has a stitch in it. It has to be a plain piece of cloth, wrapped around you, and it has to be white. King and a beggar look the same. The Koran says that's how it should be.

The Koran didn't anticipate wristwatches. Wristwatches are the only way they can show status. So you spend all your money with the most expensive, gaudy, flashy diamond gold wristwatch you can find.

Over in Afghanistan, when you're first there, you think time is important to them, because they all have wristwatches. But frequently the time on the watch says, 12:00. Time means nothing to them.

For Americans time is very precise, quantitative and serves to measure most of the rest of the world. In Afghanistan they can't believe you're wearing a Casio watch. You're a rich American, you can obviously afford a really nice watch and you've got a Casio. And they ask you why, and you tell them well it's got this function and that function and this alarm and they go, so what? What's that have to do with anything?

You'll ask, what time will we leave to go to the battle? They'll look at you like you're crazy. "We'll when we're ready."

You say, "I know you'll go when you're ready, when will that be?"

They'll look at each other like, is this guy brain dead or what? We can't leave before we're ready, and when we're ready, we will leave.

As the months turned into years, Bev grew more disillusioned about the work in Afghanistan. With her mixed feelings about the Afghani cause as well as whether the reporting they were doing was worth the illness and risk they had to endure. Especially as her fears for Hoover's safety grew, she had to struggle to integrate their experiences in Afghanistan with her life and work in the the U.S.

8 August 1983

Hi Folks,

. . . Talked to Mike about fifty dollars worth today. He's back in Peshawar. He's the David L. Dean of Afghanistan with tanks, troops, and camels—he's having a great time—a cast of thousands, vast vistas—just his scene. Hope he can remember that the ammo's live.

He was planning to spend six more weeks—(he was originally going for three total). Think I'd better get over there before he transmutes into some Lord Jim.

It sure makes Kelly seem tame. I've been working around the house . . . Been doing some kayaking to stay in shape—Although I am not sure Jazzercize would not be superior to scouring the local river bottoms with my head. Kayaks are shockingly stable upside down and the riverbottoms are appallingly close to the surface this time of year but it serves for an adrenalin rush. I see those rocks coming and start paddling upstream at a rate a salmon would envy . . . .

17 May 1985

Hi Mom,

. . . Just got back from a week in Peshawar, Pakistan. Dreadful place though the Pakis are very nice. Escaped just in time to avoid Ramadan, the Moslem period of fasting when everything is shut. I have replaced my usual Anglo-Saxonisms, like "screw you" with a far viler curse—"may you be in Peshawar during Ramadan"—which I fear will go unappreciated, but intend to use it anyway . . . .

29 October 1985

Hi Folks,

. . . Mike's packing his bags and missiles for another foray into Afghanistan. Previous survival has made him bolder which is no good. I can, at least, understand why people take these sorts of risks and it is a good cause, the best. I have also seen the results and wish he wasn't going.

. . . Giving in vitro its third and final try this month. It doesn't look good but optimism springs eternal. It certainly isn't fun, but the money runs out even before the enthusiasm. What wretched business . . . .

Mike Hoover and the "boys" on top of a "captured" tank.
". . . cast of thousands, vast vista . . . just his scene!" — Bev.
Photo from Michael Graber's collection

28 January, 1986

. . . Mike finally got off to Pakistan after a few more cancelled flights and general confusion. After he arrived the PIA—Paki Air—ticket office was blown up, killing three, wounding 29, so it's just as well he wasn't making any more adjustments.

More gun fighting in Peshawar than before. He is now able
to shoot MIGs without leaving the comforts of Pakistan as
they appear now in the Peshawar area. He's staying with General Wardok, which in some ways is good since it's heavily
guarded, but then it's the bullseye. Sure will be glad when he's
out of there . . . I feel like a creep for not going . . . .

By the late 1980s Bev had distanced herself considerably from the Af-

Bev, Mike Hoover,
and Graber
Hitching a ride in
Afghanistan.
Photo from Mike
Hoover Collection.

ghanistan work. She was doing more independent projects. She was sent
by ABC to cover some human interest stories for the winter Olympics in
Sarajevo. Arriving several months before the Olympics began she was able
to meet and befriend several of the workmen building the Olympic Stadium
in Sarajevo. Together they would all enjoy a relaxed lunch in the unfinished
Stadium. Once Beverly asked in German, what would happen when the
present leader of Yugoslavia died. The men all agreed, in good humor, that
they would have to kill one another. Soon after the Bosnian war began,
Sarajevo was reduced to rubble, the men were true to their word. Through
her work Bev could bear witness to the tides of history personally, and
experience the vast range of humanity as she moved constantly through
international and cultural borders. She also had to bear the burden of that
witness, exposed to the deep hatred and violence that is also the mark of
the human race.

"I CAN ONLY WRITE AROUND THE EDGES..."

In 1986 an American woman named Karin Wiemberger joined some of the productions in Afghanistan. Karin had lived and worked in Jackson Hole, Wyoming, doing outdoors films. She had also studied in Pakistan and knew Urdu, the official language of Pakistan. Hearing about Hoover's involvement in Afghanistan she went over to Hoover and Bev's place in Kelly one night and introduced herself. Hoover was intrigued and told Karin that though the team would be filming in Afghanistan, they would be based in Peshawar, Pakistan, and if she was near there she should come join them.

Karin received a State department grant to continue her language study in Pakistan and, after completing her training in 1986, she met up with Mike Hoover, Mike Graber and Ron Peers in Peshawar. Over the course of several trips to Afghanistan Mike Graber and Karin became very close. Graber also saw the developing friendship between Karin and Bev. Graber sadly recalls the course of Bev's relationship with Karin as well as his own:

> Karin worked with them in '86. Bev was in Pakistan and had trained Karin to do sound. Karin knew a little bit, but Beverly pretty much taught her how to do it.
>
> Bev was Karin's mentor. Karin was different, she was very comfortable about who she was. She was very much out of the Beverly mold, as I was more like Hoover. She was extremely bright like Bev.
>
> Bev had a very technical kind of mind, and Karin was really extremely gifted and strong. She was a real good trooper, just never complained, you'd *never* hear her complain.
>
> Then in 1987, I went to Afghanistan with Karin and Hoover. That was the year they were first starting to use the Stinger anti-aircraft ground to air missiles shot at the Soviet planes. Karin and I

went over, first by ourselves, and then Hoover came over and met us, to film these things being used in a combat situation.

I really liked her, and we became close friends on that trip. Then we went over again in 1988 to film, but not much was happening, and so it was a very disappointing trip. We were waiting around for things to happen, and we just weren't in the right place at the right time.

But Karin and I hit it off really well so it was fun, even though it was like 115 degrees. We loved working together, and she loved the area and spoke the language.

We were going out but we didn't want Hoover to know about it because he'd think there was a conflict, with us working together—that we'd be distracted from what he wanted.

Karin. Fully dressed to work. Michael Graber photo.

That fall Graber got a job shooting a video for Nike, and Karin went back to Pakistan without him, with another Hoover crew. That crew included Karin, Ron Peers, and two "green" or inexperienced crew support people. Their objective was to get coverage of an operation designed to cut off a main thoroughfare.

Soon after arriving in Afghanistan, Karin and Ron Peers, each accompanied by a "green" crew member, went to cover different sites. After about a month Peers became concerned because he had not heard from Karin. When the opportunity arose, he and his partner traveled to meet up with her team. By the time he finally joined up with her it was clear to him that she and her partner were sick, although this alone was nothing out of the ordinary in Afghanistan. All four continued working through the next day until, while looking at Karin through the camera lens, Peers recognized the jaundice in Karin's eyes as hepatitis. They decided to leave and get Karin to medical help. Unfortunately, they would have to cover a long distance by foot and camel before they could reach roads where a jeep could travel.

Two days later they were still on the road towards the border. That evening Peers and Karin went to their tent to sleep. After about two hours Karin woke up screaming. When Peers asked what was wrong, in her delirium she slapped him, collapsed into convulsions and then went into a coma. Rushing as fast as possible with the ailing Karin, it was still two more days before they were able to reach roads where they could travel by jeep. Even then they were not able to use their headlights due to the light-sensitive bombs the Soviets were using. Traveling in a caravan of jeeps, whenever they became separated from their caravan, Peers and the two new crewmen were forced to intermittently turn on their lights to find their way. Each time they turned on their headlights, they were subjected to a barrage of bombing. With Karin unconscious in the back seat and the two terrified neophyte combat journalists in the front, Peers struggled to maintain Karin's now labored breathing. Often she went into convulsions. Finally her pulse stopped. Ron tried CPR until it was clear his efforts were fruitless, and he had to face the fact that she was gone.

MJ, who was working for Bev and Hoover at the time, recalls with pain and frustration, her understanding of Karin's death:

> Sort of the rule of thumb was you didn't stay in behind enemy lines for more than six weeks because your food source would run out, and your health would get worse. But Karin was a pretty strong individual, and had a sense of urgency, to get that shot on film.
>
> By the time the crew caught up to her, the hepatitis had set in, it was pretty bad. She was getting sick while she was there, and there was no way to see that she was coming down with hepatitis. There were no mirrors, you can't look in the mirror.
>
> Imagine yourself up in a cave, go be in the Great Basin somewhere, go be out two hundred miles south of Salt Lake, that's what it's like out there. There's no bathroom to go look in and say, "Oh, I see I'm urinating blood." This is a very harsh, harsh climate.
>
> When the other guys caught up with her she was yellow, she was just feverish and jaundiced. You know when your old cats suddenly die,

you ever have the vet describe that? The kidneys shut down, they overdose on toxins.

For Beverly, Karin's death meant the loss of a real friend and a respected colleague. On receiving the news of Karin's death, Mike Graber was devastated and guilt-stricken for not having gone on the expedition. MJ told Bev about Mike Graber and Karin's relationship. Just as Bev had worried for Mike's safety each time he had gone over, she empathized with the pain Graber was going through and reached out to him.

Karin. Michael Graber photo.

Graber remembers:

I think I appreciated Bev the most after Karin died. Beverly wrote a letter to me in a situation where she clearly was as upset as anybody and I know that she was as wracked by Karin's death as was I. But that she would take the time to write me a letter, take the time to try and cheer me up, and tell me that she was concerned for me, I think at that point, I probably appreciated what she was like, or who she was, or I felt that I got a picture into her soul, more than before.

From Bev's letter to Mike Graber:

16 December

Dear Michael -
I would have written a lot sooner, but it just keeps coming out of a bunch of words struggling to say the unsayable.
About Karin I can only write around the edges . . . .
Please remember that Karin didn't want protecting. She was furious with [General] Wardok for not letting her go where the action was.

If she had been a whiner, she would have lived. If she had been less brave, less determined, she would have bagged the whole thing long ago. So many of the things you loved, that we all admired . . . if only, if only . . . .

I just wish there was something in this word jumble that would make it a little better for you. Time makes the pain less though it never really goes away. In a sense it is good that it doesn't. To forget is to lose the only sort of immortality worth having, which is a place in the heart of those you loved.

Anyway, I can make no sense out of death. If I can help in any way, please call.

Beverly J.

* * *

Hoover and Bev's relationship felt the stress of their work in of Afghanistan as well. In 1984 CBS had aired footage taken by Hoover of *Mujahedeen* battle movements and a bombing attack by a Soviet plane. In 1989 the *New York Post* accused Hoover of choreographing the attack shown and of incorrectly identifying a Pakistani plane as a Russian jet. Consequently claiming Russian involvement—when there was none—increasing the chances of a international conflict.

CBS and specifically Dan Rather were also taken to task for airing the alleged faked footage. Despite murkey evidence for the allegations and the fact that *The Wall Street Journal* had declined to publish the same story printed in the *Post*, the accusations received a flood of press. *The New York Times* carried several stories over a two month period covering the debate. Hoover remembers;

The headlines were: "Dan Rather fakes war in Afghanistan," and underneath in small print it said, "according to the *New York Post*."

Beverly and Hoover dealt with the negative press differently and it was around their varying attitudes that other differences surfaced.

During the height of the coverage they had received about a "hundred calls a day," recalls Hoover, which they left for the answering machine to pick-up. Hoover claims the incident, "almost didn't affect me at all," but Beverly was disturbed by what she saw as malicious and incorrect reporting. It was the fact that Beverly let the barrage of accusations upset her that aggravated Hoover. At one point they were driving out of Kelly together when Bev broke down crying, frustrated at all that was being viciously said and assumed. Hoover with his tolerance already waning describes how he "flipped out."

I got instantly pissed at her.

She's whining and crying because the press had ruined her day and now she's going to ruin my day.

I said, "Listen, there's no way anybody can wind your clock, except you. I can't make you unhappy. Only you can make you unhappy. I can make you unhappy if I take your finger and I bend it back and forth, but if I don't touch you, if I just say things to you, it's up to you to get worked up. You make my words bother you. If they're not people we like, care about or respect, what do we care what they write?"

Michael Graber, Karin and Afghan fighters. Photo courtesy of Michael Graber

She didn't get that. I just went, "You don't get it, you don't get it at all."

She said, "But you've done this and you've tried so hard."

I said, "That has nothing to do with anything, that's *their* problem, they can believe anything they want, they can say anything they want, all you can do is what you know is right and just go ahead and do your thing and whatever they want to do or believe or write, it is their problem, not our problem. For us to get involved in it and try to control what they write or try to straighten them out or something like that, no, that is not our headache, it's their's. You know what you believe and you know what happened and you know when you were there. If you're the only person in the world who knows how it is, then that's how it is, and you can tell them and if they believe you or they don't, whatever"

From very early on when we started telling this story we started getting flak. If you hit something in news that stirs something up, you should be flattered.

"Thank You for Being Patient with Me, I'm Not Usually One to Flip Out Like This"

In 1990 Beverly and Hoover returned to Antarctica to film an expedition for *National Geographic*. This was to be the realization of Hoover's original Antarctic dream.

The preparations these trips required had become routine for Bev, but still were no less taxing than a marathon. She would stay up for several days with no sleep as she went through each item they would take, repairing, preparing and often fabricating the extras they needed. It was only after they cleared customs that she would collapse on an airplane seat, for the duration of a thirteen to fifteen hour flight.

On one occasion, during preparations for this 1990 Antarctic trip MJ was working with Beverly, and she recalls having some bad premonitions about the expedition. Most nerve-racking was that Bev was uncharacteristically tense:

> When we were prepping she was the most tweaked and tense I've ever seen her. She didn't usually get tweaked. Hoover had taken off to see someone about something that needed immediate care, before the trip. It was eleven o'clock at night and her sewing machine kept breaking. Bev started to cry. She was cursing and crying at the same time . . . .
>
> I came over . . . and I said, "Go upstairs, go to bed, and I'll wake you up in three hours."
>
> She didn't. She went back to her office, and I just left her alone. I just kept packing and finally went to bed.

When I got up the next morning—three hours later—there was a note she had written; *"Thank you for being patient with me, and I'm not usually one to flip out like this."*

I didn't like it because her confidence was shaken.

Every time they go on these trips—being around them—I would just blatantly talk about, "Oh yeah, they're flying down to Punta Arenas, and then they'll go across the Drake passage." We're talking the swiftest waters, and the worst weather in the world.

With their sense of confidence about it, I had confidence in them. How could you think that Beverly Johnson would not come back from some sort of plane flight?

Graber will tell you, if you had to pick ten people, if this entire world shut down and there were only ten people left, she'd be on the team, not because she's wonder woman, or somebody strong enough, it was just everything about her.

So that's why her breaking down bugged me so much.

In addition, before she left, Beverly had been suffering from an eye problem. According to Hoover, an eye surgeon had incorrectly measured her eye for a lens replacement she required, leaving her with 400/20 vision in her right eye. She was consequently unable to focus a camera or legally fly a plane. She had difficulty reading and driving and suffered from headaches brought on by the disparity between the vision of her two eyes. Though she hated the idea of suing she had reached a point where she threatened legal action.

After much frustration and haggling and too many doctor's visits, Bev was able to have the problem corrected, but the whole ordeal was a badly timed hassle.

The Antarctic team included Hoover, Beverly, Mike Graber, Ron Peers, and Janet Kellum who had worked with Hoover and Bev on the *Survival of the Fittest* series. Janet, an athletic blond had been a cross-country ski racer and was known for her strength and physical endurance. There was also Murphy, Bev's dog, who was treated as another family member. Finally, there was Giles Kershaw with whom Bev's friendship had continued to deepen over the years. In Antarctica, Giles was an aviation legend. For flying in snowy conditions Mike Graber called him "the best in the world, the King." Giles thrived on bad weather and this trip was an opportunity for Giles and Bev to fly together, over the Antartic they both loved.

The team left in early January, and was to return in late April. The first leg of the expedition took them from Punta Arenas at the southern tip of Chile, by sailboat, to the Antarctic peninsula. Both Beverly and Mike Graber were continually seasick. For Janet Kellum, the sailing was more pleasant. She had never been to Antarctica and wrote about her first impressions in her journal.

Murphy was treated as one of the family. .
Mike Hoover photo

Wednesday January 31st 1990.

Bev came down below and woke me at 4:00 am. The Peninsula was ahead and just visible. A soft violet, rose color on a vast horizon. I'm really glad she cared enough to wake me . . . Beautiful light, a clear morning. I don't believe that I'll experience anything quite like this again. So beautiful, so free . . . crystalline, magical, endless.

The team unloaded onto the ice in a spot that Giles, who had scouted ahead in his plane, had picked out for them. For all involved, simply getting onto the ice gave them the mental boost of finally getting started.

Over the years Bev had continued her pilot training, obtained her instrument license and began experimenting with gyro-copters, which are lightweight modified helicopters that can be disassembled for transporting, and then reassembled on location. They are very delicate, and piloting one is like being a rider in the skull of a giant insect. Janet Kellum, who rode as a passenger said; "Flying in a gyro you feel so incredibly vulnerable but so incredibly invincible. It's spectacular and it's got to be the closest thing to feeling like a bird."

Bev made the first successful flight on that expedition, and in doing so became the first person to fly a gyro-copter in the Antarctic region.

The expedition also had specialized sleds, KIM snow-boards which are attached to windsurfing sails and are capable of speeds over seventy kilometers per hour, to move most of the heavy technical rock climbing supplies and camera equipment.

Giles and Bev assembled the gyro-copters and conducted a series of flights helping to navigate and transport gear from where it had been unloaded to the basecamp. All the necessary flights were completed when Hoover, Graber, and Peers set out towards a nearby peak they were planning to climb and film.

Beverly, Giles, Janet and Murphy stayed in the camp below planning to haul loads five miles to the base of the climb. The night before it had stormed and when it cleared, the ice began moving as the temperatures changed. With the ground around them cracking, moaning, and fracturing the group spent the remainder of the night hurrying to shift their camp to a more protected spot towards the edge of the ice.

Janet was in awe of the Antarctic at night:

> It was about one or two in the morning. It was absolutely beautiful out. It started snowing, big flakes, huge gentle flakes, and no wind. I'll never forget, as we went back and forth with our sled loads we were like little penguins. We had some lanterns lit and with the snowflakes coming down, it was an incredible sight.

The next morning Bev, Janet and Giles awoke at basecamp to a gorgeous clear day. The wind had not returned so there was a thin layer of fresh snow blanketing everything. Giles suggested they take advantage of the beautiful weather and fly the loads over in the gyro-copters rather than haul them by ski sleds. They also planned that Giles, who would fly in the double gyro with Janet and take the first load, would fly by the peak to check on the climber's progress. He would return to camp, pick up Beverly and together they would fly by the peak again to film the climbers from the air.

Giles and Janet loaded up the gyro and made sure they had clear radio contact with Bev. Giles completed his pre-flight. As they went to take off however, the new snow, which had begun to melt, suctioned on the gyro's skis. Janet was troubled, "we had trouble getting off, and to me it just felt kind of weird."

Once the gyro took off and stabilized in the air, Giles and Janet had a picture perfect flight and landed at the peak's base. Giles prepared to take off again, to retrieve Beverly.

Up on the peak Graber, Hoover, and Peers were enjoying the clear day. Graber recalls a gust of wind, and ice crystals blowing off the summit. The temperature was a little below freezing and from the spot they were in they could see the ocean beyond the ice fields and peaks in the distance.

The climbers had reached a high point when they heard sounds which alerted them that something had gone violently wrong below. Both Hoover and Graber remember the next sequence of events in the slow-motion detail that heightened awareness and adrenalin demand in an emergency situation. Graber was struck by the clarity with which he could hear everything.

Giles. Michael Graber's photo

Sound travels down there like no other place, because there's no other ambient sound other than wind. We could hear the gyrocopter coming in and heard it land. Then we could hear it trying to take off again, and we heard this damn thing going back and forth on the glacier, this kind of high pitched insect-like whine. Then it would wind down and then a few minutes later we would hear it attempt to do it again.

This went on for maybe ten or fifteen minutes and we heard it get airborne, and then we heard it crash.

The engine suddenly let out this scream-like high pitch. The propeller had sheared off and there was no resistance on the motor. We could just hear this metallic whine, this screaming from the motor and after maybe 30 seconds, it seemed like an eternity, it finally stop.

We looked at each other recognizing, without having to say anything, the sequence of sounds. What that said to all of us was that it was a bad accident. Because any pilot on a crash would have killed the engine. They wouldn't want the parts flying around, they don't want the fuel getting pumped, so any pilot that has any strength left will push a kill button once they crashed.

The fact that we heard that motor just screaming after the crash meant to me that the pilot had probably been killed, and possibly a passenger as well.

Now we had to climb a ways down to get back to the glacier and when we got to the base Hoover said, "Graber, you go, you have first aid training, you leave right now and go and see what you can do. Ron and I will pack up the equipment and come right behind you. I'm not sure I want to know who was flying."

Which to me meant that he thought that Beverly was in the wreckage and he wasn't sure that he could handle it.

Hoover tells how, gripped by fear, he sent Graber ahead and then had to settle himself for what he believed was ahead:

I said, "Get down there right away," and also in case it *was* Bev I kinda didn't want to go down. I was pretty certain that Bev was the one who crashed.

So I went very slowly, and was very, very weak. I would go a few feet and sit down and rest, I was very shaken.

Years later, he tried to explain how he felt:

From the time I was a little kid I had always believed I had one magic wish, and if it were reasonable, not like "I wish I could fly," I would get the wish. This idea served me well as I got older, because sometimes you might say "I wish for that," but as you put it in perspective you will say; "It's not that important." And you come to realize that the only thing you would use the wish on probably, was if your kids got in trouble physically. But you never use the wish for yourself or, "I wish I could be President."

It was a very good perspective tool that I had, and half-assed belief that it would actually happen. So as I was approaching the accident site, I just made my wish. "I hope Beverly's OK."

Rushing to the crash site Graber did not know what to expect. He says:

I took off at a sprint down through these crevasses and these steep ice sections, and then turned a corner and saw a figure walking on the glacier and as I got closer and closer and could see it was Janet.

From where she was standing on the ground Janet had watched in horror as the delicate gyrocopter flipped over and smashed into the ice about 100 yards away from her. As the motor died she was enveloped by the overwhelming silence of the Antarctic. Gathering her courage she grabbed her first aid kit and ran towards the crash.

Graber ran to reach Janet near the crash:

Giles flying over Antarctica. Michael Graber photo.

When I got up to her she said, "I'm not sure, but I think Giles is dead."

I walked up to him and I could see he was dead. He wasn't breathing and his eyes were open. I put my thumbs on his eyes and closed them.

I had to wait for Mike and Ron Peers to come down.

Up on the mountain Hoover caught a glimpse way out on the iceberg of two distinct figures walking toward the crash site below. He recognized one as a person, and the other as a dog. He knew then it was Murphy walking with Beverly and that she was alive and safe. His wish had been granted.

As one by one the team members arrived at the crash site, the day's events came into focus. After dropping off Janet, Giles had tried to fly back across the glacier to basecamp to get Beverly. He was unable to get the gyro-copter off the ground, so Janet helped him tinker with the controls as he tried to figure out the problem. She suggested that she ski back across to the basecamp, and Giles could follow her taxiing the gyro, but Giles was determined, and finally he was able to get the craft to take off.

Watching him from the ground Janet saw the gyro reach an altitude of about 200 feet and then simply turn over and plummet to the ground. At the time it was unclear what caused the gyro to flip although everyone noted erratic wind shears over the next several days.

Up on the mountain Hoover caught a glimpse way out on the iceberg of two distinct figures walking toward the crash site below. He recognized one as a person, and the other as a dog

Back in basecamp, Beverly had been waiting for Giles to return. Spurred by the sinking feeling that something was wrong, she put on her skis and started off for the base of the peak, arriving and to find her friend dead.

The aftermath of the tragedy was a macabre series of events. Graber recounts his experience of the days following Giles' death:

At this point we were all pretty numb, we were all buried in our own self-pity. It was always, "We have to notify Annie Kershaw, his wife, but we can't call out on the radio," because Giles was basically a legend in Antarctica and any phone transmission—radio signals— would have been monitored. The word would have spread out across Antarctica and probably would have gotten back to his widow before she was officially notified.

So there was a dilemma over how to deal with this so that Annie would be able to find out first hand what had happened.

What followed was certainly one of the most bizarre weeks in my life.

That evening there was a beautiful sunset. Giles had been talking, while we were down there, about how he hadn't seen a real good sunset, and that this far South, sometimes, you would witness fantastic twilights but no real sunsets, and on this particular night there was an incredible crimson sky sunset, golds, reds and pinks.

Hoover and Bev, got on the radio and called the *Sol*, our support ship. They requested the boat to come and pick us up. That was all they could really say over the radio. The crew of the boat came in, it took them a day to get back. We then loaded Giles' body on a sled and brought it back over to camp, and later onto the boat. We told the crew of the boat about Giles' death and they were all upset and blown away. Giles had an amazing charisma about him.

Ron Peers and I stayed in the camp to keep it from being destroyed by the winds. The rest of the crew sailed off on the *Sol* and went to a British base where they could reach Annie Kershaw, and notify her of her husband's death.

The boat came back and they unloaded Giles' body again.

What happened was, Annie had decided that since Giles loved the continent so much, he should rest on the continent. Furthermore Annie was going to fly down in a couple of days and have a funeral for him here.

They also unloaded this wooden casket that had been made by carpenters on the British base. This casket was pretty big and heavy. Now in our little camp, we had Giles' dead body *and* this casket.

We're stuck. Where could we bury him? We couldn't bury him in a hole in the snow because when the weather warms up, the snow would melt and he would just melt out, right? The only bedrock was up on the mountain on the glacier where we had climbed earlier.

So we took Giles, wrapped up in a plastic bag back, on the sled and skied him back across the glacier. We kept the body in the ice overnight by placing it in a cravasse. We knew that Annie would want to see Giles face so we packed extra ice around his face.

We climbed up the mountain and found a flat place. Then we started moving rocks to make a suitable gravesite for him, and then we went and got the casket.

We got the casket the next day and we were sledding it back across, and there was one section of the glacier that was full of crevasses. Suddenly a gust of wind blew the casket right off the sled and down into one of the crevasses. Now we have this empty casket in a crevasse.

But after the accident—in our haste—we had left all our climbing ropes up on the climb. What were we doing without any ropes? It was actually kind of hair ball, since we had no way of rescuing anybody.

So we improvised, we tied bootlaces together. I found a narrow section of the crevasse and climbed down, found a floor, and walked along until I reached the casket.

Meantime the people above lowered down this rope of bootlace which I tied around part of the casket, then I climbed and pushed, and they pulled from above. I am certain it was the first time in mountaineering history that anyone had ever rescued an empty casket out of a crevasse with bootlaces.

So we got the casket, and put it in place, and skied back to our camp.

Next day Hoover and Beverly started really early because they were planing to carry Giles' body up to the the burial spot, which was about 100 yards from the crevasse he was in. The Twin Otter flew in, and in it was Annie Kershaw, looking just like someone who's just heard her husband's death, and had hopped on airplane and flown for maybe 70 hours straight to get to Antarctica, to see his body one more time before he's buried.

There was a Chilean Catholic priest, and a couple other people who hopped off the plane right behind Annie. They unloaded two other boxes that weigh about 75 pounds each.

Janet lead them all across the glacier to where Giles body was.

I looked down at these boxes and I picked them up. "This must be a carved headstone," because I could not imagine what would be that heavy in wooden boxes. I said, "Oh no, they'll need these for the service."

So I skied back to camp, got a sled, came back with the sled and loaded these two heavy boxes on the it, then tore off across the glacier trying to catch up with everyone so I would not miss the funeral. I got over just below where the funeral is. I unloaded the boxes and took an ice ax to open them thinking, "I'll just carry the headstones from here."

They were filled with powdered cement! Someone had sent the cement from Chile thinking they would need it. Where was anyone in Antarctica going to find the water to make the cement?

We buried him there and piled rocks over the casket and then piled rocks up to hold the cross in place.

With Giles' death the plans for remainder of the expedition and the conclusion of the film had to be re-organized. They had to coordinate with everyone involved in the expedition, each reacting in their own way to Giles' loss. Hoover had his own understanding of what should be done and made it clear that was how things should go:

There were three schools of thought about finishing the film. There were the realists, "You know it's dangerous, you know when you go out on these things you might not come back, and you're not doing it to find a cure for cancer or anything like that, it's a very selfish thing, so if you get yourself killed, really nobody should feel sorry for you."

The realists would be headed by Giles if he were alive, Graber, and myself. Giles was flying around in some goofball machine in some faraway place, and gets himself killed, he wouldn't want anyone to feel sorry for him, he wasn't like that.

The second school was the typical airheads, "Oh God, oh no, I had no idea it was dangerous!" These people who are so surprised and think it's such a tragedy. That school was primarily the twelve people on the boat. They had already almost gotten stuck, and had been very close to being sunk, the weather was turning bad, the days were getting shorter, Giles gets killed, and all of a sudden, these people go, "Wahhh, it's dangerous. We could get killed down here!"

They had thought it was some sort of a lark?

Then the third school, that was only Beverly. "Let's put things in a bigger perspective. We have X number of people here, they believe that they want to do this, and they have ideas and concerns and worries, and their ideas etc., should be heard, and the democratic rules, whatever the most people want to do, we should do."

Of course she and I were at complete odds on this.

Independently the crew on the ship decided it was time to leave and radioed Hoover and the expedition team to tell them to get ready to be picked up. Unfortunately for the captain, as Hoover said, "Well, he didn't have any idea who he was talking to, he hadn't a fucking clue."

Hoover continues; "Is that so?! I had NO idea that this was a democracy, but apparently it is. I thought it was absolutely a dictatorship and I was the dictator. How silly of me not to know that you and the crew can tell us what to do by some *vote*, how silly of me not to know that, of course that's how it is. So this is what we're going to do, Chris (the Captain). You pull anchor *immediately* because it is so dangerous down here. I don't want you to spend an extra second in the Antarctic because you just might get hurt. So I suggest you sail immediately for Chile, we will stay down here and do what we have to do."

Then I just hung up.

Then Bev says, "No, I don't think that is right," and Janet Kellum says, "I don't think that's right either," and Ron Peers says, "No, things are bad, the handwriting is on the wall, let's get out of here."

I said, "Ok, you guys know where the boat is. See ya," and Bev was shaking her head.

So then just Graber and I went, we went on alone. The others had their choice, "If you're not here when we get back that's your choice, see ya."

Graber and Hoover went and finished the climb and the filming while the others remained in camp. Bev composed a press release which described the events during the expedition for the public. This is her first draft:

PRESS RELEASE (1st draft)
ICE 90

The twelve member "ICE 90 Expedition" returned to Punta Arenas the end of last week. [The expedition was sponsored by the National Geographic Society with logistic support from LAN Chile.] After completing over two months of filming in the Chilean sector of Antarctica, the mountaineering team sailed north on the 200 ton—thirty three meter—schooner "SOL."

The primary goal of the expedition was to explore a route onto the Arrowsmith Peninsula and then attempt to find a way through the elaborate crevasse field which surrounds the Needles—a spectacular range of near vertical mountains. This region is east of one of the oldest bases in all of the Antarctic—the Chilean base—Carvajal which is located at the southern end of Adelaide Island. If the Needles could be reached, the team would then try a first ascent of the spectacular unnamed granite spire. To do this, the team was composed of technical rock wall climbers from Yosemite Valley in California.

In early February the expedition's ship "SOL" managed to off-load the climbing and filming team onto the fractured ice shelf near Blaiklock Island . . .

From a basecamp on the ice shelf, the team set up two very small gyro-planes which are similar to an ultra-light helicopter They were brought down to help find the route through the complex crevasse field known as Checkerboard Mesa, and then survey the mountain range.

By the end of February, the gyrocopters had found a route and the ice team had managed to move their advance camp and supplies into position below the spectacular spire.

The final assault on the mountain began the first week in March. As the climbing team moved forward, one of the gyro-planes, flown by Captain Giles Kershaw, climbed into the air to help the assault team find the best and safest route to the top. Then, very suddenly, a freak Antarctic catabatic wind came silently down off the interior icecap of Antarctica and hit the little gyro-plane, flipping it over and slamming it into the ice below. Giles Kershaw died in the crash. He was 42 years old and had flown more hours in the Antarctic than any other pilot in polar history. Giles Kershaw is credited as the man most responsible for opening up the interior of the Antarctic to non-government operations and was one of the founders of Adventure Network International and Antarctic Airways—both of which operate with their Chilean partners out of Punta Arenas.

Giles was buried on the side of the mountain, which the team named in his honor. Mike Hoover, the expedition leader, said of his friend that "Giles had spent the last 17 years of his life exploring the Antarctic and he never tired of its powerful beauty. His body will will become part of the land he loved and taught so many other people to love. His spirit is everywhere here."

During the next several weeks the climbing team was unable to proceed partly due to very strong winds which made any travel impossible. Two-meter high snow block walls were constructed around the tents to keep them from blowing away and an emergency snow cave was built in the event that the tents were lost to the high winds. The "SOL" radioed that the winds were causing the ice shelf to break up and that the team would have to return immediately to the ship.

Then, on March 16th, there was a break in the weather and the winds began to drop. Mike Hoover and Mike Graber, both veterans of Mt. Everest expeditions and two previous Antarctic climbing expeditions, made a push for the summit of one of the more dramatic Needles on the Kershaw Pinnacles. On March 17th, the two man team climbed straight through the previous high camp without stopping, and then weather turned completely calm and the sun came out. Mike Hoover led onto the summit ridge and then Mike Graber took over and traversed out onto the vertical rock face which lead to the summit. At 1305, March 17, 1990, Mike Graber set foot on the top with Hoover soon to follow. According to Mike Hoover, "It was almost magical how the weather cleared for us . . . . and we tried to see the magnificent view as Giles would have. Wonderful, but it still hurt."

The entire team will be returning to the United States and the film of the expedition will be shown as a one hour special on the National Geographic Society's television series "Explorer." The film will be shown in Chile through LAN Chile this coming spring.

After the accident Graber was aware of a change in Bev. He said:

You could see Bev hurting, the spark just wasn't in her eyes. Beverly, in my estimation, had really been hit hard. Giles was a very special friend for her. They had been through a lot together, done a lot of flying. They had flown together from the United States to Antarctica.

She was like I had never seen her. She was really devastated by it. Nonetheless, she was always looking for, "What do we have to do next?" She would never allow herself the luxury of self-pity but I think of all of us she felt the greatest loss.

Though Beverly kept her pain to herself, and focused on taking care of the logistics for Giles' funeral, completing the film and finishing the expedition, the wound Giles' death made was deep, and Beverly did not recover quickly.

On the sail back to Punta Arenas, Murphy gave birth to a litter of puppies. Murphy's presence next to the distant figure on the ice had represented to Hoover that Bev was alive, and Janet Kellum remarked that Murphy's new puppies "in a strange way were a reminder that life takes but it also gives." She added, "It was a trip that took more away from you than it gave."

"When We Look at the Glass, it Is Not Just Half Full, it Is Overflowing"

Bev didn't slow her pace in the aftermath of Karin and Giles' deaths, but she was forced to look again at how much of her life was beyond her control, up to the whims of forces much greater than she was. One autumn day she and Malinda Chouinard had the opportunity to go for a short hike—with Murphy following them along—and reflect on all they had lived through. Malinda recalls their conversation:

> While we watched the dog play in the creek, we recalled Bev's many mishaps keeping up with and leading the guys . . . We wondered why Giles was killed and not her in that gyro-copter, or on the motorcycle chasing camels when she hit the barbed wire. We both barely survived ectopic pregnancies, she hiking for help in debilitating agony, never again to conceive that much longed for baby. We wondered who would slip away next, and talked about the short space between the quick, and the dead.

Bev focused some of her concerns on broader social and humanitarian issues. In the wake of the Yellowstone fires she wrote a letter to an editor which displays not only her political views but her recognition of the ties between environmentalism and business.

Editor:

The torrents of hysteria that gush across the pages of this paper will not revive a single tree in Yellowstone. It's time to quit despairing and visit the park.

You will see a devastated park, the hand of nature at work or an additional tourist attraction, it's a matter of attitude like the half full/half empty glass. You may come to believe that lodgepole pine forests are not one of the great scenic wonders of the natural world (utter heresy) and that, in any case, much forest remains as it was. You may be reminded that Yellowstone is more than trees: it is geysers and animals, cliffs and canyons. Or you may just feel plain sick. Or outraged. What is important is to see for yourself.

Take a picture of your kids in front of a burn, take one next summer when the grasses start to grow, and the year after and the year after Yellowstone will not be the same in our lifetime or in our children's or in their children's but it will still be wonderful and wondrous, alive and growing.

Talk to people from out of state. The ones I talked to were fascinated by the fire. Give them your business card and make sure that they take a picture of their kids by a burn.

Don't forget to pick up your free firewood on the way out.

Perhaps you will find that the glass is more than half full.

Once we have seen for ourselves that Yellowstone is still there, it will be easier to convince the rest of the world. In this matter we are not receiving much in the way of outside assistance. The stream of dignitaries proclaiming the park destroyed doesn't help, no matter how genuine their concern. It's hard to imagine Ronald "you've seen one redwood, you've seen 'em all" Reagan being much help. Trying to assign blame and exact punishment will only reinforce the idea that what remains of Yellowstone is smoldering snags. Disaster aid suggests an even grimmer scenario.

On the other hand, the Park Service which, fortunately, is no longer claiming that this is the greatest event since sliced bread, still has a fellow on the loose proclaiming the fires have produced a wonderful new habitat for wasps and woodpeckers. The NPS should make every effort to apprehend and muzzle this individual, since wondrous though they are, wasps hardly warrant a drive from Kansas.

Finally, we should remember that the National Parks do not belong to Jackson, or Livingston, or Billings. They do not exist for our benefit. While we can and should question park policy, we should realize that the answers may be that what is best for the park may not be what is best for us.

But, never mind, visit the park. Perhaps you will find the glass is more than half full. When we look at the glass, it is not just half full, it is overflowing.

Though she could appreciate and savor the world around her, her own life, her microcosm, continued to contain much pain, physical and emotional. After returning from Antarctica, Bev and Hoover went to make a climbing picture in Timbuktu entitled *Off the Wall in Timbuktu*. After weeks of reconnaissance and pre-production, the group of climbers and film crew flew to Africa to begin filming. They had settled into camp one evening only three or four days into the trip when Bev decided to cook some French fries as a treat for everyone. She began to boil speanut oil on the open fire and as she was moving around the fire she stepped on the corner of the pot and the boiling oil spilled over her foot. She suffered terrible burns on her foot and ankle and there was no ice or even spare water for her to use against the pain. They shipped her to the local hospital. Within ten days she returned to the team, on crutches, to try and help out however she could. Bev suffered from the pain from the burn but also the pain of humiliation of getting injured. She understood that in getting injured she was jeopardizing the entire expedition and

Mike Hoover photo.

the filming. Hoover was furious that Bev had been so clumsy.

On expeditions like that, said Hoover, you not only have a responsibility to take care of yourself for selfish reasons but you have
a responsibility for the whole group. Her going out early on in the
expedition leaves a huge, huge gap to be filled.

Bev would feel badly about it in any event, but from my selfish
point of view, you're making French fries or something, which is
really nice but an absolute luxury, and fooling around doing that
conceivably could have wrecked the whole expedition.

Some people get hurt more than other people. I don't get hurt,
but other people do. You watch the way they do things, how they
think and they are just accident prone. Beverly was accident prone.

Same with equipment, you break one piece of the wrong equipment, it's over. And it has never happened on one of my productions.
Primarily for one simple reason, I am a tyrant.

Dropping something and breaking something, it doesn't matter
how sorry you are, I don't even care about that. Beverly dropped a
camera once on *Survival of the Fittest*. It came within about ten feet
of a whole group of other cameramen below, and it would have
killed them. I don't drop cameras, but Beverly was a little scattered.

So that was a very hard trip, to a large extent because we didn't
have Beverly. She was the strongest part of any expedition.

Working together over so many years, doing what needed to be done
for every expedition, learning the ways Mike Hoover wanted things prepared and taking care of details before they could become problems, Bev
had become Hoover's third eye and third hand an essential part of him.
But this meant she was wife, partner, lover and at the same time colleague,
business partner, and teammate. She was the buffer between this temper and
the rest of the world, and also the first in Hoover's line of fire.

Bev and Graber over the years had come up with a code so that when
Hoover was in a good mood, Bev would tell Graber that Hoover had taken
his "Mister Roger's pill." Graber was at the receiving end of many disputes
with Hoover and though he loved Hoover and saw him as a mentor there
were also long periods when the two were not on speaking terms.

In 1992, Bev and Hoover began working with Bruce Brown on the feature film, *Endless Summer II*, the sequel to Brown's 1960's surfing documentary hit, *Endless Summer*. Bruce Brown, speaking in 1995, his skin weathered from years of sun and ocean water, his blond hair bleached to luminescence, describes Bev's role during the filming:

> Mike would give her a hard time a lot of times, it's not like man and wife, it's like sound person and camera person. She never looked rattled, but I could see her hands sort of shaking. I'd go, "Mike, Jesus, back off, leave her alone, she will figure it out." She would never say anything.
>
> He would say; "Ahhh, shut up."
>
> You would never get her to say anything bad about Hoover.

Ultimately though, Bev was Hoover's wife. Did she dismiss his outbursts as part of who he was? Her whole life Bev had pushed herself to her physical limits, and at times beyond them, did some part of her agree with Hoover's criticism?

On the *Endless Summer II* shoot Bev was excited about the professional opportunities that came her way. Bruce Brown asked her to film one surfing sequence herself in Texas, where there was a wave machine. She was the only crew member to travel to every different location. The rest of the crew was grateful for the experience Bev had with fixing the equipment. Bruce Brown was awed at her ingenuity:

> If the camera malfunctions she'd be taking it all apart in little pieces, soldering it all, putting it back together. She'd have her little miner's light on in the middle of the night. Didn't matter if you were in the middle of the jungle or some hotel.
>
> I remember in Hawaii it was a plastic lid on the Nagrine, it was warped so it was touching the reel. She went and got some sand from the beach, and put it on the stove and heated it up and poured it on the lid, molded it with the hot sand, put the lid back on and it was fixed. I'd be saying, "Pretty clever, huh guys?" She never mentioned it.

Bev also found a few moments to enjoy where she was, and even try a little surfing. One morning in Costa Rica she went out to the ocean with a surfboard at the crack of dawn. When the rest of the crew awoke they couldn't find her, until someone spotted her drifting out in the surf, fast asleep in the growing sunlight.

In 1992 Hoover and Bev returned from filming in Costa Rica to a city full of fire and wrath, Los Angeles after the Rodney King trial. They rode through the decimated neighborhoods and talked about how the hope for a future free from the violence around them depended on the opportunities for the children.

Hoover and Bev had researched adoption and Hoover especially was very interested in adopting an older child from Afghanistan:

> I went to Pakistan and Afghanistan because I was hot for adopting a child. Beverly wasn't that hot for adopting. But I knew how she was. You would say, here, this is your kid, and she would love the kid, it wouldn't matter if it was hers or not.
>
> We wanted an older kid, two or three, or even four. The biggest problem is that because it's a rabidly Islamic country, you're taking an Islamic child and giving it to a non-Islamic parents. So when it came time for even our close friends to sign off on it, in a way it's bit of a death warrant for them, not literally a death warrant, but it would be a black mark against them. Anybody they were in contention with for anything could say, "Do you realize this person would take an Islamic child and given it to infidels?" That's the way they think over there, they're very vengeful.
>
> So we were told, "Just become Muslims, or just pretend to be Muslims, we don't care, say you are Muslim, sign on the dotted line, you're Muslim and everybody is off the hook. If later on, they found out you were lying it's not our problem, you said you were."
>
> So that was their idea, just take care of it that way. Beverly and I said, "We can't do that, it's a bad way to start out this, with a big lie like that." And it is not something to take lightly.

So the next approach was to get Muslim, Pakistani or Afghani people in this country to adopt the child, and then transfer him to us. What kinds of legal problems we'd have we had not investigated yet.

MJ speculated that not having children intensified the isolation from other women Bev had known back when she began to climb:

I think deep down inside she felt the aloneness of it.

Her other friends whom she'd started out with, Malinda Chouinard, Susie Tompkins, all knew each other from the climbing days, and yet Beverly continued to climb while other woman friends got married, had families, and the common ties with them were less and less.

She was not stuck doing what she was doing, . . . had she been a traditional or even semi-traditional wife, or business woman or mother . . . but Bev went on a different direction.

Beverly was a business woman, it was her business, but she was not dealing with the rest of the world in a businesslike manner. It wasn't the type of business where she had to attend to on a daily basis. Beverly was living a life of adventuress.

Most of us have our adventures in our twenties, by the time we are in our thirties our adventures are, "my god what is he going to say today?" That is an adventure, just a different type. I think for Bev there was a feeling of "does anybody really understand?"

I wish Karin was still alive because I think that's how the two of them would have stayed close, continued on in their friendship.

"Read My Lips, No Pain"

Hoover had just returned from his trip to Afghanistan looking into the possibilities of adopting a child when, on April 1, 1994, he and Bev took off for a long weekend of backcountry heli-skiing in the Ruby Mountains of eastern Nevada. It was an annual event in which they were joined by their many friends including Clint Eastwood, whom Hoover had worked with in the *Eiger Sanction*, and Dick Bass and Frank Wells, whom Beverly had helped in their attempt to climb the highest peak on each of the seven continents.

This trip would be the first opportunity Bev had had to ski on her newly reconstructed knee.

In 1993, while skiing with Hoover she had torn the ligaments of one of her knees and had not been able to ski for a year. When the accident happened, Hoover had been skiing in front. He made a big jump and then stopped below to wait for Bev. She was close behind and as he watched her prepare for the jump he saw her ski come off leaving her at the brink of this small cliff with only one ski on. He remembers that he could see her leg twist, almost in slow-motion, and the pain register on her face, as the ligaments were completely torn. She survived the cliff and then put her other ski back on and skied slowly to the bottom of the hill. At the doctor's office they examined her and when they asked if she'd come in an ambulance, she explained that she had driven there herself. She was unable to ski for the next year, had had reconstructive surgery, and had to wear a brace much of the time.

Bev had been battling with residual pain from the injury ever since, but now she had finally reached a point in the healing where the pain was completely gone. As she skied the first day of the trip to the Ruby Mountains she was free from the constraints of a bruised and battered body. Hoover recalls:

They finally got her knee to work real well, and had it so that two days before the trip to the Ruby Mountains she was in heaven, her knee was so perfect.

While we were skiing I would frequently come up to her and say, "How's the knee, how's the pain?"

She'd say, "Read my lips, no pain."

"Yeah right, you always say that."

"No," she said. "There is NO pain. Not even a little bit."

And her smile was just huge. She loved it so much. She smiled twenty-four hours a day.

Bev was beaming from ear to ear. Each time the helicopter put them down on the side of a peak, the Ruby Mountains were spread out around her. Cold, clean air filled her lungs and she looked out over the open view, the descent ahead; opportunity, anticipation, the comfort of good friends. Then she would tilt her skis down the slope, let gravity take her, and fly off into the wilderness again.

"Enjoy this Day"

Bev spent her time on this earth living passionately, not waiting to die, and therefore it seems appropriate to leave her in a moment she was vibrantly alive. But death is the conclusion of everyone's story; Bev's only came sooner than anyone wanted.

On April 3, 1994, one day before Bev's forty-seventh birthday, the group of back-country skiers awoke to gloomy weather.

Hoover, Bev and Frank Wells and a few others were eager to get in some skiing despite the weather. The helicopter pilot, Dave Walton, whom Bev had worked with on the Yosemite helitack crew, said he thought he would be able to find a way to fly. But, as they got ready to leave the weather deteriorated and he reconsidered. They all agreed that tractor skiing would be a better option. They would use the tractors as a mobile ski lifts to return them to the summit after each ski run. The snow was beautiful fresh powder, and the smaller group of only seven, (which included Hoover, Bev, Frank Wells, Dick Bass, Kevin Wells, Kevin's girlfriend and a few others including some local guides) was more intimate. The skiing was through trees, Bev and Hoover's favorite terrain.

After having lunch in the ski hut the group got word over the walkie talkie that the weather was going to close in and that the helicopter was going to come in to pick everyone up while it was breaking. If they didn't leave soon they'd have to take the tractors out which would take much longer. The first helicopter in was a Lone Ranger, a big model, and, "everybody scrambled to get on board" Hoover recalls. But Bev and Hoover had a policy of being the last to leave, in part because they had faith in their own survival skills. If there was a chance that the other helicopter couldn't make it in, they knew they could ski out. Frank Wells and Paul Scannell, another friend, decided to stay back with them.

The second helicopter, a smaller model, came in. Frank Wells got in the left side, Bev, as the smallest climbed in the middle because there was a bulkhead there, then Hoover got in on the right. Paul Scannell sat in the front with Dave Walton in the pilot's seat.

Everyone was in a good mood and listening in on the headsets, but just after they took off, the bad weather closed in. They flew along the range, unable to get down below the weather. Finally Dave was able to find a spot to put the helicopter down in order to wait for the weather to blow over.

Hoover remembers that after they landed he asked Dave if he wanted to cover up the intakes, but Dave declined, explaining that he thought they wouldn't be on the ground very long. Hoover got out of the crowded helicopter to stretch and take some pictures while the snow continued to fall.

When Hoover returned to the helicopter everyone was beginning to feel the cold. Dave fired up the engine to get the cabin heat going. He ran the engine for about twenty minutes or so and everyone warmed up and dried their gloves on the cabin heater. Then he turned the engine off. There had been no problems.

They continued to wait. Intermittently Dave would talk to the crew down at the lodge below. From their lower elevation they could see the weather patterns and could tell Dave if there looked to be any breaks in the weather. Finally they said that there was a clear patch coming up and Dave got ready to try and catch it.

Dave and Paul got out to clean the snow off the helicopter. Hoover went to help. "I don't know enough to know what he's doing, but I could see he was spending the time up there," said Hoover, also noticing that Dave had checked through the intakes. Together the three removed all the snow from the helicopter as best as they could, at one point Hoover held Dave up on his shoulders while Dave got the snow off the boom. Then they all climbed back in and took off.

Within two minutes after take off it was clear something had gone wrong. Hoover, sitting behind Dave, was taking photographs over Dave's shoulder and noticed the attenuator lights on the dashboard go on. These flashing lights indicated serious problems: the engine had gone out or there was no oil pressure. Mike Hoover heard Dave on the radio telling the crew below that they had an engine out and were going to have to "go in," that is, make an emergency crash landing.

Hoover leaned back and told Beverly the engine was out and she should brace herself. Beverly leaned forward, and being a pilot immediately understood the meaning of the flashing lights. She braced herself for the crash. Hoover told Frank about their situation but, "Frank couldn't believe it, he was saying, 'What, What does this mean!'" Hoover remembers. Looking out the window—Hoover thought that with some maneuvering on Dave's part, the landing would not be too bad—and let Bev know that he was not too concerned. Hoover figured they were not that high and not going that fast, "No big deal," Hoover recalls thinking.

Mike Hoover was wrong. They were not high enough to maneuver into a good landing spot and as the helicopter hit the ground Dave was killed instantly and Paul was injured by a tree which pierced through the front of the helicopter.

Hoover never lost consciousness completely but faded in and out of a stunned fogged state. He says, "I didn't think the accident was that bad, I could hear moaning and stuff. They pulled me out and I remember that my elbow hurt real bad but nothing else hurt." Hoover was taken from the wreckage and leaned against the helicopter. The rescue team had left the lodge below as soon as they head the helicopter was having trouble, and reached the accident within moments of the crash.

As he lay against the broken helicopter Hoover began to understand the severity of the accident. He says "I knew that it was bad because of their hushed voices." Hoover could hear the rescuer's sorting through the wreck, evaluating the victims one by one, "He's gone . . . he's gone . . . he's gone," and then . . . . "She's gone." Beverly died at the scene from head injuries.

Paul and Hoover were the only survivors of the crash. Because of the severities of his injuries, Paul was taken in the first helicopter to the emergency room in Reno. Hoover was taken next. Everyone else was dead. Paul lived for nine more days before dying from his injuries. Hoover sustained fractures to his neck, skull, shoulder, right elbow and his rib cage. His left ankle was crushed. He stayed in the hospital in Reno for three days and then was taken by air ambulance to a hospital in Wyoming, where he was treated by his regular doctor. After a year and a half of recuperation it is still unclear if his foot will need to be amputated. The exact cause of the accident will most likely be settled in a courtroom.

In 1995, MJ Koreiva recalls what it was like to see Beverly's body at the mortuary:

> I sat with the coroner at the mortuary, and went through all this. The look on the poor mortician's face—he kept looking at me, questioning—because he was just been going over this body that's got scars all over it.
>
> This is not a battered wife, I affirm.
>
> I had to go through, this is El Cap the first time, and that one, because she had one eyelid that was a little low, in fact I took the stitches out on that.
>
> That was the day we were taking all the bricks off the roof. She said, "Will you take these stitches out?" I said, "Oh yeah, sure."
>
> This was just recently, and then because they did this there was a scar here.
>
> On the fingers, on the knees, on the foot, that was the hot oil in Mali when they were going towards Timbuktu.
>
> And right, that's the camel round-up on motorcycles in the middle of Australia.
>
> You could tell a story by looking at every finger or limb, and all I could do was sort of sit there and chuckle.
>
> Bev would have done the same thing.

For many people the amazing things about Beverly were what she herself took for granted. MJ remembers that Studs Terkel talks about "the extraordinary acts of ordinary people." Bev thought of herself as ordinary; she never thought she was super-human.

She had asked that if she was killed she not be given a huge gravestone, but rather, if it would satisfy others, a small plaque laid somewhere with a simple phrase on it. "Something," she wrote, "like 'Enjoy This Day.'"

It is appropriate that a woman who had a simple faith in herself and her life should write her own conclusion. Bev left behind a letter to be given to her parents in case she was killed. Although it did little to soothe

the pain of her loss, this letter offers the sincerity of a woman who deeply appreciated her time here. Her life was epic not because of what she accomplished, who she met or where she went but because she valued, throughout the pain and the loss her experiences, her life and her loves. In this gratitude is the fuel of her afterglow, the importance of her memory. Her letter said in part:

Dear Folks,

. . . I have had a wonderful life . . . and up until now at least I have been very lucky. Lucky enough to have you as parents. Lucky enough to be born in America. Lucky enough to be healthy. Lucky enough to have two excellent brothers . . .

. . . I have had about as much fun and adventure as it is possible to have. I have loved and been loved. I am sorry that I haven't done much for the improvement of the planet but that was the next phase. Rather poor planning on my part. Otherwise I have lived enough for 100 years, it just got a bit compressed.

I have appreciated every day and marveled at what a wonderful and mysterious thing life is. I do not look to any further life, but this one was life enough . . .

. . . So my last request, my only request really, is that you not let this make you even a little bit sad. I have had all out of this life anyone could ask for and more. If you can think of me and smile . . . that is what I really wanted.

Think of me and smile. . . Photo by Mike Hoover

The Beverly Johnson
Memorial Scholarship Endowment
Fund for the Teton Science School

This fund was established in 1994 by Mike Hoover, Doreen and Ed Johnson, and members of their families, and includes contributions donated in honor of Beverly's memory by friends and business associates.

The income from the fund will be used to provide scholarship for economically disadvantaged Junior High School students, most specifically but not limited, to children from the South Central Los Angeles area. The scholarship is intended to cover the full costs for the child (or children if enough funds exist) to attend a two weeks session of Teton Science School summer program.

If you wish to make a donation, please contact:

Executive Director of the
Beverly Johnson Memorial Scholarship Endowment Fund
c/o Teton Science School
P.O. Box 68
Kelly, WY 83011
or
Call: (307) 733-4765
Fax: (307) 739-9338

The Author, Gabriela Zim and her faithful companion Scout.
A Graduate of UC-Davis is following on the footsteps of her grand mother Eleanor Goddard Worthen and her mother Helena Harlow Worthen. With this, her first book, she is now the third generation women in her family to be published. Photographed by Julie Feinstein.

MOUNTAIN N'AIR BOOKS publishes fun books.

We specialize in adventures, and we love good food. Here is a list of our books in print. If you wish to purchase any of these titles, and they are not immediately available, please ask your local bookstore manager to order it for you.

ADVENTURE GUIDES:

Cross Country-NORTHEAST
A guide to the best cross country skking and inns of New england and New York
John R. Fitzgerald Jr.
ISBN: 1-879415-07-0 $12.00

Cross Country Skiing in Southern California
A guide to cross country skiing, touring and telemark descents in Southern California.
Eugene Mezereny
ISBN: 1-879415-08-9 $14.00

Great Rock Hits of Hueco Tanks
Over 120 of the best routes of this rockclimbing winter destination.
Paul Piana
ISBN: 1-879415-03-8 $6.95

Mountain Bike Adventures... MOAB, Utah
A travel guide and resouce index for traveling to Moab, Utah with the mountain biking family in mind.
Bob Ward
ISBN: 1-879415-11-9 $15.00

The Rogue River Guide
A kayaker's guide to the beautiful wild and scenic Rogue River, located in Southern Oregon.
Kevin Keith Tice
ISBN: 1-879415-12-7 $15.00

ADVENTURES, LITERATURE:

High Endeavors
The best of Pat Ament. A collection of mountaineering essays by one of the best American rock climbing authors.
Pat Ament
ISBN: 1-879415-00-3 $12.95

A Night On The Ground, A Day In The Open
The story of a poet, a visionary, a real mountain vagabond hard at work.
Doug Robinson
ISBN: 1-879415-14-3 $19.00

On Mountains & Mountaineers
A two-way mirror between the mountains and the writers that bring them to life, in the pages of mountaineering literature.
Mikel Vause
ISBN: 1-879415-06-2 $12.95

Rock and Roses
The first mountaineering anthology published in the United States of America on wish all contributors were woman mountaineers and rock climbers. Critically acclaimed.
Mikel Vause, editor
ISBN: 1-879415-01-1 $11.95

COOKING (Bearly Cooking):

Cooking With Strawberries
Many delicious ways to serve fresh or preserved strawberries.
Margaret and Virginia Clark
ISBN: 1-879415-26-7 $10.95

HIKING & HIKING GUIDES:

Backpacking Primer
Tips, tricks, techniques, and step-by-step help on outfitting and organizing a successful backpacking trip.
Lori Saldana
ISBN: 1-879415-13-5 $12.00

Best Day Hikes of the California Northwest
The best short hikes of the California Northwest.
Art Bernstein
ISBN: 1-879415-02-X $13.50

Best Hikes of the Marble Mtn. & Russian Wilderness Areas, CA
16 selected trails, 137 destinations and 93 trout fishing lakes
Art Bernstein
ISBN: 1-879415-18-6 $16.00

Best Hikes of the Trinity Alps
The best shor and not so short hikes of the Trinity Alps, in northernmost California
Art Bernstein
ISBN: 1-879415-05-4 $17.00

Portland Hikes
Hikes in Oregon and Washington within 100 miles of Portland, OR.
Art Benstein, and Andrew Jackman
ISBN: 1-879415-09-7 $18.00

OTHER GUIDES:

The Nose Knows;
A Sensualist Guide to Great *Joints*. A restaurant Guide for Pasadena, Glendale, Burbank, The West Side and the Greater Los Angeles Area. Restaurants serving dishes for under $10.00.
Lloyd McAtter Battista
ISBN: 1-879415-23-2 $13.00